Creative Dance
in Grades Four to Six

Creative Dance
in Grades Four to Six

JOYCE BOORMAN

Academic Press Canada Limited

"Achoo!" from *Fluid Filosophies of Future Fools* by Bob Dyck. Reprinted by permission, Professional Printing Ltd.

Extract from "Point Grey" from *Legends of Vancouver* by Pauline E. Johnson, reprinted by permission of The Canadian Publishers, McClelland and Stewart Limited, Toronto.

"Bon Dance" from *A Pepper Pod: Classic Japanese Poems Together With Original Haiku by Shoson,* by Kenneth Yasuda. Reprinted by permission of Alfred A. Knopf, Inc. Copyright by Kenneth Yasuda.

"Gentle Willow" from *A Pepper Pod: Classic Japanese Poems Together With Original Haiku by Shoson,* by Kenneth Yasuda. Reprinted by permission of Alfred A. Knopf, Inc. Copyright by Kenneth Yasuda.

Selections from a fable by Jean de la Fontaine, reprinted by permission, New English Library Ltd.

"The Tide in the River" from *Silver Sand and Snow* by Eleanor Farjeon. Published by Michael Joseph Ltd., reprinted by permission.

"Slowly" from *The Wandering Moon* by James Reeves, reprinted by permission of William Heinemann Ltd.

Every step has been taken to make the list of acknowledgements comprehensive; but in some cases, all efforts to trace the owners of copyrights failed. All errors or omissions drawn to our attention will be corrected in future editions.

Set in 10/12 point Baskerville

Paper: 50 lb. Williamsburg Offset

Printed and bound in Canada by The Hunter Rose Company Limited

34567   79

ISBN   0-7747-3006-4

CONTENTS

*To my mother and father in lieu
of all the letters which never
get written!*

ACKNOWLEDGEMENTS

Grateful acknowledgement is made by the author to Murray Smith. His companionship in sharing the mystery and excitement of young children has been a constant source of challenge. His belief that children need to be allowed to retain their sense of joy and wonder in the world of movement has been a continual support to those engaged in dance at the University of Alberta.

To Margaret Crawshaw of Nonington College of Education, Kent, for her constant challenge to my educational philosophy which has helped to clarify many aspects of this work.

To Bunty Clements, for her initial reading of the script and her contribution in making so many practical suggestions. For these, both myself, and many teachers are extremely indebted.

To the Principal, staff and children of Waverlee Elementary School with whom I worked and discovered so much.

To children from North Vancouver, from Dance Session '70, University of Alberta and from Saturday Morning Dance Classes who have provided many of the "movement pictures".

To three excellent photographers who waited so patiently to bring the movement to life in a cardboard frame, William Rauschning, Ann Hall, Chris Hildred.

To Terri Hanak, who has tried for the first time to meet the demanding task of illustrating a chapter on stimuli for dance.

Finally, as always, to Mrs. Beryle Campbell, without whom no book would have ever emerged.

FOREWORD

The little boy stood at the water's edge and stared intently as he dug his small toes into the glistening sand. As they disappeared beneath the surface the space above filled at once with swirling, foamy water. He crouched, completely absorbed in wonder and probed with his fingers to discover the lost toes which made a sucking sound as he straightened them out returning them to his view. He patted the water and wet sand gently at first, then with increasing vigor until he splashed wildly. Then he paused to lift a dripping hand to his mouth to taste this new delight. All at once he straightened up and shifted his gaze far out to the sunlight flickering on the quiet water of the lake. He turned and ran splashing and shouting with pure delight along the shimmering edge of the beach.

In moments like these children undergo some of the most profound learning experiences of their lives. Unfortunately, too few such episodes occur within the formal context of school learning. In this connection Aldous Huxley has pointed to the importance of education on the *nonverbal level*. He sees this as a necessary complement to the heavy emphasis in our schools on scientific reduction, relying as it does on the use of conventional symbol systems and formalized cognitive processes. He contrasts the objective world, the world of external reality, as it is organized and explained in our generally *agreed upon ways of knowing it* through "words and the stock of second-hand notions" with another, equally important but more often neglected world. That is:

> the world of sheer mystery, the world of an endless succession of 'unique events, the world as we perceive it in a state of alert perceptiveness with no thought of explaining it, using it, exploiting it for our biological or cultural purposes. As things stand now, we teach young people to make the best only of . . . (the) . . . world of familiar words, accepted notions, and useful techniques.[1]

This present volume indeed provides a practical means of beginning to swing the scale to a more appropriate balance between the

---

[1] Aldous Huxley, "Education on the nonverbal level." *Daedalus,* Spring 1962.

verbal and nonverbal aspects of education. Such a swing toward greater emphasis on nonverbal education is not at odds with the observable trends in the larger field of education. On the contrary, of the many aspects of Miss Boorman's writing that interest me as a teacher, none is more important than the beautiful consistency with the best of modern educational thought. Here are workable approaches to individualizing learning, to encouraging problem solving and creative activity, to relating movement to the many facets of life with which it is inextricably associated but from which it is too often separated. Further, the possibilities of arousing and maintaining motivation that has its sources deep within the individual learner are clearly available in her approach to this form of dance.

One hopes that we are presently witnessing several important shifts in emphasis in public education that include both the application of the fruits of research into the learning process, and attention to aesthetic elements to a degree that has never before been the case, at least on this side of the Atlantic. The practical immediacy of the difficult life of the pioneer has never really been shaken off. The puritanical, pragmatic influences from our history have largely denied us access to the enriching potential of what Huxley so vividly describes as the "endless succession of unique events."

It has done more than that. It has contributed substantially to the artificial partitioning of North American life into segments to be assigned exclusively (or almost so) to one sex or the other. In no place is this more apparent than in our traditional attitudes to male participation in the arts in general and dance in particular. Can one imagine a television serial, in which the hero, a rugged individual, (whether cowboy, private eye, lawyer or doctor) is also a dancer or violinist? It boggles the mind! How many completely healthy and constructive (dare one use the word "normal"?) boys have squelched sincere and potentially deep interests in the arts because expression of such an interest in our society could, and still can, call into question one's very maleness? What price has been paid by those who threw caution to the wind and pursued such interests regardless? As a long-time coach of football and swimming I suspect that the courage required in such cases often surpasses the demands of competitive sport for physical courage or the guts to maintain a killing pace in a tough race.

Dance is an avenue through which we can become more realistic and rational in our view of what people really are. It can help us to recognize that emotional reaction is a human response not restricted to either sex, and, as the dentist and surgeon have long known, that courage is by no means an exclusively male characteristic. We may even come to understand that compassion and gentleness are qualities whose presence would enhance human relations as much in men as in women, and moreover are not mutually excluded by the presence of such qualities as strength and even controlled aggression. What would be the effects on some of the current distortion of personal and family life if men generally were relieved of the heavy burden of feeling that they had to ride forth, alone, to battle and subdue the dragons of modern life, all the while avoiding displays of strong emotion or any hint of anxiety? One can only speculate.

Observing Miss Boorman teach elementary school boys and girls, one is struck immediately by the enthusiastic acceptance and ready involvement of the boys in particular. (The girls, as expected, take to it eagerly!) The important conclusion is that our long held prejudice about the *natural reactions* of boys to dance is a full blown myth that can be laid to rest just as soon as the sensitive teacher approaches it from an intelligent point of view.

There are many disquieting influences at work in the world today. But one influence that can only be encouraging is toward a redefinition of what the appropriate roles for the sexes really are. Let us hurry the arrival of the day when it will be legitimate to recognize and nurture genuine individual interests and personal gifts as they occur in either sex. Such a day can be considered more than the liberation of any one sex, but part of a *human* liberation in a real and important sense. A necessary step toward that end is to begin to expand the educational spectrum that is made available to *all* of our children. This book will provide a vehicle for physical education or other dance teachers interested in undertaking such a journey.

Murray Smith, Associate Professor
Chairman, Dept. of Educational Services
Faculty of Physical Education
University of Alberta, Edmonton

INTRODUCTION

The purposes of this book are twofold. First, to provide information on what creative dance is and how it can be taught in Grades 4 to 6; and second, to act as a companion volume to *Creative Dance in the First Three Grades*.

The basic content of this book stems from the writings of Rudolf Laban, his movement analysis forming the foundation of the work in dance in the elementary grades.

In endeavoring to develop this book as a continuation of the earlier one, certain difficulties were encountered. Ideally, the material to be learned in Grades 4 to 6 should grow out of material studied by the children in earlier grades. In practice, this seldom happens, and teachers are faced with presenting dance for the first time in Grades 4, 5 or 6. In such cases, the teacher has to ensure that the foundation of the earlier material is laid.

Chapter 1, in particular, looks at this problem and suggests ways of embarking upon simple movement concepts in a manner that is acceptable to the older children.

Chapters 2, 3 and 4 look at the concepts of effort, space, and relationship. They show how these factors can both be presented for the first time and how they also develop beyond the work presented in *Creative Dance in the First Three Grades*.

Chapter 5 looks at the total movement analysis and, in order that the book may be used alone, repeats some of the material given in the earlier one. This repetition is kept to a minimum, and the movement analysis is extended into material appropriate for the older children.

Chapter 6 extends the ideas on stimuli and develops further the use of music.

Chapter 7 does not include the detailed observation given in the earlier book, but looks more specifically at the practicalities of dance teaching. In this chapter, the use of transparencies is introduced; transparencies have been used with all grades, and have been found to provide a real link with the vocabulary development of students in the early grades. Transparencies have also expanded the freedom of choice in the use of action words; the visual patterns and indication of effort content in movement have added to the verbal and kinaesthetic understanding of the children.

Again, it must be stressed that the teacher controls the lesson plans, and not the reverse. The lesson plans given here provide a framework from which the teacher can build. They can be changed, developed, cut, or deleted, according to the needs of each teacher and class. Specific recommendations for their use are made on page 17, and teachers should refer there before reading or using any lesson plan.

Finally, I must reiterate my belief and faith in the value of creative dance as part of the child's total educational development. Working with children is not always easy and many problems are encountered—but these problems are not really different for teacher, practicing student, lecturer or professor. Gradually, with each group of children, the difficulties are ironed out and dance does become a very vital aspect of the child's school life.

Joyce L. Boorman
Edmonton, 1971.

1

INTRODUCING CREATIVE DANCE

Creative dance, for both children and teacher, starts from the known. All children are familiar with the actions and sensations of running, skipping, leaping, hopping, collapsing, balancing, spinning, pouncing. Sometimes they have used these actions intentionally; other times a mood or an idea has set them whirling into an action of which they are not really conscious. In creative dance these actions, which are already so familiar, will have to be transformed from the functional to the artistic. This does not happen immediately and it will not happen for all children at the same time. Even having occurred, this awareness will disappear, hopefully to reoccur at some later stage.

This functional material with which one starts on the road towards creative dance, can be termed "action words". Like colours, these words can be shaded to many different hues. As blue can be softened, hardened, deepened, lightened; so too can turning become whirling, twirling, swirling, spinning.

A simple grouping of action words will help the children and the teacher as they discover the difference between moving and dancing.

ACTION WORDS   Action words can be grouped only in a general sense but these groupings can help the teacher and the children understand the essential quality of the action and the word. The grouping can also help the children to clarify their activity when they have changed the essential quality of a word and used it to express something different from its original nature. For example, a leap can generally be placed in the "jumping" group, but when a child deliberately emphasises the travelling aspect of the leap, an entirely different movement expression occurs. Children and teachers should, therefore, be aware of (but not bound by) general groupings of words.

Single Action Words

Travelling Actions

run	slither
skip	hop
creep	gallop
rush	dart
flee	

Vibratory Actions

shiver	shake
quiver	tremble
wobble	vibrate
patter	shudder

Jumping Actions

leap	hurl
toss	bound
prance	bounce
soar	fly

Turning Actions

spin	whirl
twirl	whip
swivel	

Stopping Actions

freeze	hold
perch	grip
anchor	pause
settle	

Percussive Actions

stamp	punch
explode	pound
patter	

Contracting Actions

shrink	shrivel
close	narrow

Expanding Actions

grow	reach
release	open
spread	

Sinking Actions

collapse	sink
lower	drip
fall	

Rising Actions

lift	rise

These groupings then form the foundation of the action words upon which creative dance is built. They become the environment which the children explore, and with which they create. The words can be explored singly or they can be developed into sentences of action.

Sentences of Actions

patter—freeze.
run—toss—grip.
perch—twirl—gallop.
tremble—freeze—dart—explode.
explode—whirl—settle.

These sentences of actions can be developed in a purely exploratory way before any attempt is made to create, design and formalize a finished movement sentence or dance sequence. Such exploration can be developed by:

a) using the same words in different order:
toss—perch—twirl—run.
run—toss—twirl—perch.

b) reversing the order:
whirl—freeze—flee—explode.
explode—flee—freeze—whirl.
c) changing the rhythm of the sentence by repeating one word:
toss, toss, toss—perch—twirl—run.
d) changing the rhythm of the sentence by:
changing the timing from sudden to sustained,
changing the force from firmness to finetouch.
e) changing the rythm by increasing and decreasing the size of the
actions.
f) changing the articulation of the action by emphasizing or using
different body parts. Perch can be explored on the feet, seat, shoulders, knees. Twirl can be lead by the head, the palms, an elbow.

When exploring any of these changes the teacher should take care
that they are logical. For example some words already have within
them a quality. It is the quality which is the essence of the word.
"Toss" has the quality of lightness or finetouch. If you change the
lightness to strength it is no longer "a toss" but more like "a throw".
If, in changing the quality, the children do completely change the
action, then the new action should be recognized.

3

All of the action words and sentences of actions can be explored with a variety of sounds and in a variety of situations.

The children can create their own sentences of action:

a) in silence,
b) with voice accompaniment,
c) with body sounds, e.g., clap,
d) with percussion,
e) with partners or in small groups,
f) with recorded music.

The first of a series of lessons in creative dance can be based upon the foregoing material.

INTRODUCING ACTION WORDS TO GRADE IV

Before children in Grade 4 have been exposed to creative dance they will already be familiar with, through both speaking and writing, many exciting action words: i.e., creep, fly, fall, whirl, explode, collapse, linger, hover, shrink, shrivel, hop, gallop, leap, jump, tumble, roll. For them, words can already evoke mood, emotion and a picture of action. They will consequently take to working, physically, with action words as the proverbial "ducks to water". They delight in physical action and sensation.

The following six lessons can be used in any order. They are set out in this particular order to give the teacher guidance in some of the many ways children can be introduced to creative dance through *action words*.

Lesson 1

Material of the lesson / To explore action words. Bounce—(two of children's own choice) Roll—Spin—Run, individually and in groups of three.

GUIDED EXPERIENCE

1. *Everyone find a space. Ready? Bounce, bounce, bounce and freeze. Again. Bounce, bounce, bounce and freeze.*

2. *Try to make your bounces very light and resilient; as if the floor is made of sponge rubber.*

3. *Let your bouncing action carry you from one place to another but always after three or four bounces. Freeze for a second or two before starting again.*

DISCOVER

Go into groups of three and try to find two other action words which have a bouncing quality. When you have found those two words, as a group, try to perform them.

4

Possible action words here would be—hopping, bounding, rising and sinking.

OBSERVATION AND QUESTIONS A short time could be given here for observing the results of the children's group work and the following questions would be important.

1. *What was the main quality or sensation that you found in bouncing?*

2. *How did you try to show this quality in the actions you chose to do?*

The main qualities in bouncing are the light resilient feeling in the body and the continuous pattern of a rising and sinking action.

GUIDED EXPERIENCE 1. *Here are three action words which do not "bounce". Spin—roll—run. Try and put those words into a sentence of action—you may use them in any order.*

The children will require time to explore these words before proceeding to the next stage of the lesson.

OBSERVATION *Return to your original group of three and first of all watch each other to see in which order you each used the words spin, roll, run. Take it in turns to show each other.*

5

DISCOVER   1. *In your threes make a group shape close together.*
2. *All starting at the same time, perform your own sentence of spin—roll—run, as you travel away from each other. At the end of your sentence, freeze.*
3. *Repeat your sentence. This time travel back towards each other again and freeze in your group shape.*

CLARIFY   *Repeat the idea of starting as a group, travelling away—freezing—traveling back towards each other—freezing in a group shape.*
Again the children will need considerable time to work out this idea and they should be helped in making the following discoveries:
1. That in order to finish at the same time, they will probably have to speed up or slow down some of their actions.
2. Instead of speeding up or slowing down, they might extend some part of their sentence; e.g., make two or three rolls instead of only one.
3. They might have to shorten one of their actions; e.g., not run so far.
4. If they do not arrive back in their group at the same time, the first one to arrive back will have to hold on to their positions.

FORMULATE The lesson should end with each group being able to formulate a
very short sequence of action words in which they show that they are
also beginning to be aware of each other as members of a group.

NOTES TO THE TEACHER

1. The beginning of each lesson should have a rhythmical activity
which immediately sets the children working, and involves them in
both activity and a flow of movement.
2. The sequence of "bouncing" and "freezing" in groups of three
was a fairly simple situation for the children in which they could
work easily as groups. The second situation was given to present them
with a far greater challenge in group adaptation. It may be necessary to simplify this situation for a particular class.

Lesson 2

Material of the lesson / To explore, through individual and group
work, the action words and movement sensations of leaping—lingering—weaving—contracting.

GUIDED EXPERIENCE 1. *Shake one leg until you feel it vibrating. Shake the other leg and
make it vibrate.*
Repeat this rhythmically several times until you feel sure that the
children's legs are really warm and relaxed.
2. *Imagine the floor is one gigantic trampoline. Start with one fairly
small leap and then, because of this trampoline floor, let the leaps
take you about the room.*
3. *When you are on a trampoline you really feel suspended or as if
you are lingering in the air—try to get this quality into your leaping.*

DISCOVER *Try to find out as you are leaping what it is that helps you to stay
longer in the air.*

GUIDED EXPERIENCE 1. *Take any sitting or kneeling position in which you feel comfort-
able and the top half of your body can move freely.*
2. *For a few moments feel yourselves breathing very deeply and
breathe in and out quite slowly.*
3. *This time as you breathe in and out let the top half of your body,
or an arm and hand, accompany the breathing with a rising and
sinking action.*
4. *Feel, particularly, the movement at the top of the rising action.
You feel "suspended" by air before sinking again. This is like blow-*

7

ing the air into a balloon. When the air is blown in, the balloon expands and rises, when the air is let out, the balloon sinks and grows smaller.

DISCOVER   *Try your leaping actions again and see if you can extend the moment when you are lingering or suspended in the air.*

GUIDED EXPERIENCE   *1. You have probably, at some time or another, watched, and even tried to catch, a butterfly. Imagine the delicate up and down whirling flight of the butterfly. As you follow it with your eyes and your head, try to use your leaps to help you catch it in your hands. Don't harm it!*
Give the children several moments to now work with this added imaginative idea.
2. Now follow this butterfly, but, instead of leaping to catch it, follow it with running, pausing and creeping actions. These actions make you weave, in and out of each other, round and about one another, as you follow your own butterfly.

DISCOVER   *Go into groups of five and together try to work on this idea of leaping, running, pausing and creeping, as you combine in the search of the same butterfly.*
Again allow the children time to work on these ideas.

GUIDED EXPERIENCE   *1. Everyone for a moment sit down and watch my hands. I am going to very gently and cautiously bring my thumb and my finger tips together.*
2. Now you try. Keep the quality very delicate and slow; as if you have in your hands something very, very fragile.

DISCOVER   *See if you can bring your group together in a closing action which has the same delicate, careful quality.*
Again, time should be given for the children to work with this idea.

FORMULATE   *From the beginning, as a group:*
a) Leap, search for your butterfly.
b) Intertwine and weave as you follow its path.
c) Very, very carefully and gently, as a group, close in on the butterfly until it is captured without being harmed.

NOTES TO THE TEACHER

1. To get the feeling and quality of staying in the air, the children need a good take off, where they really use the strength of their legs to propel them into the air. Once in flight the head and the upper

parts of the body should be lifted upward; but without any look or feeling of strain.

2. It is essential in all lessons that the teacher remember how important the hands are for the children, in capturing the quality of an action which cannot as easily be conveyed in words. Hands are for the teacher an invaluable teaching asset.

Lesson 3

GUIDED EXPERIENCE

Material of the lesson / To explore a combination of sound and action in phrases which move and stop.

1. *Everyone fetch an instrument and then come and make a loose group near the center of the room.*
2. *Find a position in which you can comfortably sit and at the same time use your instrument quite freely.*
3. *Altogether we will now make a sudden short burst of sound and then, immediately following the sound, every instrument is silent. It's very similar to when you do an action and pause; now, instead, you all create a sound and then silence.*
4. *Watch my hands the first few times and I will indicate the sound and the silence.*

DISCOVER

Without my help can you now make your sound go and stop by simply being sensitive to when the sound is going to stop?
Allow the children time to respond to this situation as it requires considerable awareness of the whole group.

GUIDED EXPERIENCE

1. *You have been creating sounds which go and stop. Now think of any action which also goes and stops, such as: run, jump, spin, hop, shiver, roll. Once you have thought of your action get up and try to accompany the action with sound, and the pause with silence.*
The children explore for as long as the teacher senses the need for the learning in this area to continue.
2. *Now reverse the idea; you make no accompanying sound when you move, but give an emphasis to the stop by creating a sound.*

CLARIFY

Decide which way you are going to use your instrument. Either:
a) *to accompany the action with sound, or*
b) *to accompany the moment of stillness with sound.*
Once you have decided, make a sentence in which you repeat the same thing three times, for example:

whirl—stop
whirl—stop
whirl—stop.

9

This time think of a sentence of three action words. It might be hop —shrivel—roll. Decide which two actions you will work with a sound accompaniment, and then work the other action word in silence, for example:

hop—sound
shrivel—silence
roll—sound.

Once you have tried several different ways, make a decision to stay with one idea which you like, and work upon that until you have really mastered it.

This lesson will require considerable skill in observation on the part of the teacher, in order to estimate how long to leave the children exploring each experience. The children should not be rushed through the above experiences because this one lesson is the starting point for many developments with percussion and action words.

NOTES TO THE TEACHER

1. This way of introducing percussion has been mentioned briefly in *Creative Dance in the First Three Grades*. With the older children, however, it can be developed further, allowing them the opportunity to explore the sensitivity of responding to a group sound without any external "conductor". For the older children this adds a further challenge.
2. In this lesson children are being given some of the ways in which they can explore the "togetherness" of sound and action words. No great "dance" creations are likely to emerge, but the children should be given the necessary time to explore, what is a comparatively new medium for them—accompanying their actions with an instrument.

Lesson 4

Material of the lesson / To continue with the exploration of action words and percussion.

1. *Everyone fetch an instrument and then go and sit with others who have the same type of sound.*
The children will normally go into drum groups, cymbal groups, bell groups, and castanet groups. If there are any further sound categories the teacher may have to help the children to decide which group has the nearest similar sound.
2. *As a group choose two action words which you think most closely describe the sound of your instrument. For example, the bell group might choose shivering and prancing because these are light, delicate actions.*

3. *Once you have chosen your actions make a short sentence with them, moving towards and then away from each other.*

The teacher may find that the children, given this problem and having decided upon the two action words, work as a group or in pairs.

CLARIFY *Make a short sentence of action and sound in which you use each one of the two actions. Once you know your sentence try to repeat it.*

GUIDED EXPERIENCE *In an orchestra sometimes all the instruments are played at the same time, sometimes they are played separately. Sometimes only a few instruments play together.*

DISCOVER *Go back to your groups and decide how you can become an orchestra of sound and action. Don't play too long a "symphony". Keep it short and simple.*

The children will need a fair amount of time to get organized on this problem. The teacher should move among the groups and help with suggestions such as:

a) Keep the original sentence which each child has already created.
b) Does the "orchestra" all start playing their piece at the same moment and finish at the same moment?
c) Does the whole "orchestra" start and then some gradually stop and others continue?
d) Does one "instrument" start and the others join in?

FORMULATE *Now that you know your own orchestra piece, the whole class can become a larger orchestra.*

The teacher should then give guidance something on these lines:
The bells start—finish
The drums start—finish
The castanets start—finish
The cymbals start—finish
The whole orchestra plays at once and finishes.

These two lessons, on action words used with percussion, together with the lessons given later for Grades 5 and 6 are only a few of the many in which children can be involved in action and sound.

NOTES TO THE TEACHER

1. The anology of an orchestra is such an excellent one that most children immediately understand what it is they are striving for even if their attempts are not always initially successful.
2. The action words which the children select to put to their sounds should be similar in quality. This quality will also be affected by how they choose to use the instrument. The teacher should try to

help the children to make this correlation by carefully observing their original ideas and giving guidance where necessary.

3. If there happened to be a large group of one instrument, e.g., ten drums, it would probably be advisable to split this group into two smaller groups.

Lesson 5

Material of the lesson / The action words, gallop—shake—toss, used to the accompaniment of "The Light Cavalry Overture."

GUIDED EXPERIENCE

1. *Everyone to one end of the room. Let's see you galloping as quickly as you can to the other end of the room and back again.*
Repeat once or twice, really encouraging the children to travel and let their actions flow onward rather than being restrictive in their movements, in any way.

2. *Find a space and sit down cross-legged. Now very gently bounce, and bounce, and bounce your head forward and toward the ground.*
Repeat rhythmically several times giving the children a moment of pause between each phrase of bouncing. Then fill the pause with another action such as—*stretch upwards in your sitting position and then bounce, bounce, bounce.*

3. *Repeat the same action phrase but have your legs stretched out in front of you, either apart or together."*

DISCOVER

Stand up. Repeat your galloping action but this time travel about the room. Feel how you need to stretch your legs from the hips as you gallop.

GUIDED EXPERIENCE

1. *Listen to the first phrase of music and see if you can hear how it travels through space.*

2. *This time, when you hear the music, move with it using your galloping—travelling actions.*

DISCOVER

Work with the music again, but be aware of when you change from leading with your right side to leading with your left; or do you perhaps not make this change?

CLARIFY

Decide exactly how you are going to work with your galloping action, how many right and left changes you are going to make. Be able to repeat what you have done.

GUIDED EXPERIENCE

1. *Find a space and, for a moment, work upon isolating parts of your body with a shaking action, for example:*

12

shake one leg
shake the other leg
shake one arm
shake the other arm
shake your seat!

2. For a moment imagine a horse that really gallops like the wind, suddenly stops and shakes its tail!
3. Try to capture this quality by traveling, stopping and shaking your seat really vigorously!
It is absolutely vital here that teachers realize the essential difference between capturing the quality of the movement of the horse, and asking children to *become* horses. The latter will be discussed more fully in the chapter on stimuli. In this lesson, notice the way in which the idea has been presented to the children.
4. Listen again to the music and this time listen for the second phrase where you will quite clearly hear the "shake", "shake", "shake".

CLARIFY   *With the music, work out these two phrases, galloping and shaking.*

GUIDED EXPERIENCE   *1. Take hold of a piece of your own hair right at the top of your head and gently pull it away from your scalp.*
2. Can you feel how your head wants to move upwards?
3. Try some leaps now where you really toss and lead upwards with your head.
Give the children time to experiment with this.
4. The horse has a magnificent mane and as he tosses his head he seems to leap in the air.
5. Try the idea of shaking your tail and tossing your head to this phrase:
shake – shake – shake
toss – toss

CLARIFY   *All the way through the dance:*
galloping—really travel
abrupt stop—shake, shake, shake the seat
toss and toss the head
shake, shake, shake the seat
toss and toss the head
away into the gallop again.

The children either can listen to the music all the way through before working, or dance immediately. This is a very short, simple piece in which actions can be clearly heard.

13

1. In creative dance, the training of the body in both strength and suppleness grows naturally out of the creative work. In the first part of this lesson the children are being exposed to very simple, but specific body training. This has an immediate and relevant link with the creative work.

2. This whole dance has a tremendous element of fun in it, despite its simplicity. It would be a mistake to present it "childishly", whereas there is everything to be said for capturing "child-like" fun with your class.

Lesson 6

Material of the lesson / Use of the action words rising, skipping, hopping, jumping—running, hurtling, in a dance composition accompanied by the music "Creatures of the Garden" by Donaldson. The actions will capture and echo the "essence" of the music. The teacher should make him or herself fully aware of this essence prior to the lesson.

GUIDED EXPERIENCE

1. *Everyone come and listen to this short piece of music.*
After the children have listened once or twice:
2. *Go and find a space and start "shaking" every bit of you.*
3. *Stop! Make a rhythmical phrase of shaking and stopping but when you stop, emphasize one part of your body as you hold your shape. Maybe a shoulder, elbow, or foot.*
The teacher should accompany this activity with the drum, using a very light, sharp double beat to bring about the stop. Eventually the children are going to be rising with light, stacatto actions, emphasizing different body parts. Therefore, they should be guided towards capturing this quality in their stillness.

DISCOVER

1. *Start near to the floor and take quite a long time to rise. Try to gradually come up using very light, short, sharp movements which are constantly emphasizing body parts.*
The teacher can help the children when they are doing this by suggestions to use the space behind their body; to isolate body parts for slightly longer by using them repeatedly rather than once only.
2. *Listen to the first phrase of the music, which is the longest, and then see how your rising action fits with it. Perhaps you need to come up even more slowly although you should still be keeping all those small, light quick actions of body parts.*

CLARIFY

Allow the children to work with the first part of the music two or three times until they have this part clear in their own minds.

14

GUIDED EXPERIENCE   *1. Now you are right up on your feet the rising leads you into skip-*
                     ping, hopping or jumping actions.
                     2. For a moment let's practice those one after the other.
                     3. Ready—hopping, and hopping, and hopping, and hopping and
                     hopping. Try the other leg! Keep those hops bouncy, light and re-
                     silient. Now skipping, skipping, skipping, skipping. Try using differ-
                     ent directions and even crossing your feet over. Now jumping, jump-
                     ping, jumping and jumping. Try to keep your feet together and
                     make light, high, bouncy actions.

                     Again the teacher should notice here the importance of a rhythmi-
                     cal repetition with these activities. (She could leave the children to
                     work with each one of the actions according to their own rhythm
                     or impose a class rhythm with the drum.)

DISCOVER   *Select whichever one of these actions you prefer, the hopping, skip-*
            ping, or jumping, and find out how you can fill a very small floor
            space with your action.

            The teacher can find many ways of evoking this idea of working
            with a small space. Here the term "fill" is used with this intention.

GUIDED EXPERIENCE   *1. Now make your sentence of skips, hops or jumps, but on the last*
                     one, pause for a second, take a deep breath, then burst into a run.
                     2. Try this several times and, when you are running, weave about
                     the room using up as much space as you can.
                     3. For a few seconds try some short runs ending in a flying leap
                     that hurtles you through the air.
                     4. Sit down and listen again to the music all the way through. Feel
                     how one part slips naturally into the next.
                     It sounds like rising—light—stacatto emphasizing body parts. Once
                     up, it fills a small piece of space with skips, hops, or jumps.
                     Then, the sound of breaking out from this confined space and run-
                     ning to enjoy all the space and celebrating with an enormous leap.
                     (You will hear the run and the leap occur twice at the end of the
                     music.)

FORMULATE   Allow the children some uninterrupted time in which they can
             formulate this final dance. Some help may still be needed with the
             linking parts. The important thing is the creating of the feeling of
             the whole dance not three separate, broken phrases.

NOTES TO THE TEACHER

Before commencing this lesson the teacher should be thoroughly
familiar with the music. Although the children will be guided in
structuring the sentence of action words, the quality of the dance
can only be caught through the involvement of the teacher. If the
teacher cannot catch the essential quality of the music, she is not

16

likely to be able to guide the children into exploring this potential in the action words.

CONCLUSION

These six lessons have been given in order to provide the teacher with a few practical ideas for starting creative dance with Grade 4. In using the lessons it would be advisable to do the following:
1. Read them through several times in order to feel and understand the "wholeness" of the lesson.
2. Keep the outline of the lesson in mind but be prepared to deviate from it when advisable.
3. Simplify or expand on some of the challenges which are given to the children.
4. Make your own lesson plan from the original one. During the lesson reading your own shorthand will be easier than trying to refer to the book.
5. Use the lesson as a starting point for ideas of your own.
6. Have the action words clearly displayed for the children's reference.
7. Refer to the following references for further information:
Boorman, Joyce. *Creative Dance in the First Three Grades*. Canada, Longmans, 1969.
Russell, Joan. *Creative Dance in the Primary School*. London, Macdonald & Evans, 1965.

MUSIC USED IN THESE LESSONS:

Lesson 5: "Light Cavalry Overture" by Von Suppe. Available on Volume II, *Basic Listening Program for Primary Grades*.
Lesson 6: "Creatures of the Garden" by Donaldson. Available on *Children's Rhythms in Symphony*, Bowmar Records, Inc., No. B-2053.

INTRODUCING ACTION WORDS TO
GRADES V AND VI

These lessons are presented for either Grades 5 or 6, because in terms of "dance experience" the children will be starting at the same place. There will however be differences in the background, development, attitude and readiness level, which the children will bring to the work. Similarly, each teacher will bring a different personality and attitude to the teaching. Once again, these plans can be considered only as a guide to which each group, teacher and children together, will bring their own ideas and unique development.

The material in these lessons is based on my experiences with a particular Grade 6 class, and, although the names have been changed around, is presented in the form of a dialogue between the teacher and the students. The idea behind this form of presentation is to give the teacher an opportunity to note how the work has to be encouraged, fostered, challenged, and commented upon throughout a lesson. Some lessons give not only the material but recorded observations of what occurred. These observations show how, frequently, a lesson will develop from what has occurred when the children start to work upon a problem.

Lesson 1

Material of the lesson / To explore the actions of running, freezing, turning, jumping, sinking, rising and any further appropriate action words.

GUIDED EXPERIENCE

RUNNING AND FREEZING

1. *Everyone find a space by yourself and when you hear the drum beat run very swiftly about the room. Stop.*
Repeat this activity several times in order to ensure that the children are relaxing and responding to an unknown situation. Vary the length of the phrases: This helps the children to become mentally and physically alert.
2. *Repeat the running and stopping but this time when you stop, take a position that is quite low down near to the floor and very strong.*
Repeat several times.
3. *This time when you stop, take a position that is high. This position should be pulling you away from the floor.*
Repeat several times.

FORMULATE

This time when you stop, select whether you will be high or low.
Repeat twice.

GUIDED EXPERIENCE

JUMPING

1. *This time without any drum accompaniment let me see you leaping, almost hurling yourself, into the air.*
Allow time for the children to work with this. At the same time move amòngst them. Comments such as "Good, John", "Oh, come on, you can push harder than that!", "Try it with a turn", will help the children.
2. *Everyone sit down except Kim and Don. Would you two show us your jumps?"*

3. Watch for the difference in these jumps.
4. What are they? Right, Kim turns in the air and Don travels a long way in his jump.
5. Is there any other differences? No?
6. Kim and Don, would you do your jumps once more and this time everyone watch how they land. Yes, Mary?
Kim lands on two feet at the same time. Don lands one foot and then the other.

FORMULATE   *Everyone up and do your own jump three more times trying to remember how you did it.*

GUIDED EXPERIENCE   *1. Everyone find a position very near to the floor. When the drum*
TURNING AND COLLAPSING   *is beaten continuously and softly, make a turning action which pulls you away from the floor; when it is beaten in a very sudden rhythm, quickly collapse down to the floor again.*
Repeat this sequence several times rhythmically.
2. Good. Now let's try to improve that turn by making it very much stronger. As you turn try to think how you would move if you were pushing something heavy up towards the ceiling. Just try the turning action on your own for a moment without any drum accompaniment.
The children are given time to work at this.
   Children often find a great difficulty performing a strong action. They will be helped in this by being told to keep their seat very firmly positioned directly above their legs, or not to let the seat stick out. This is a very tiring action and should not be performed for too long.

CLARIFY   *Everyone take your position near to the floor and again make a sentence of turning and collapsing while listening to the drum accompaniment.*
Repeat sentence three times.

FORMULATE   *You have worked upon five action words: run, freeze, jump, turn, collapse. Now I want you to try something different with these words. I will accompany the running and freezing on the drum. I will repeat three times. Then I shall stop drumming and you will continue with your own jumps. Repeat your jumps three times and let the last one bring you into a low position near to the floor. Once I see that everyone is in that position I shall start the soft continuous drumming which means you will start your turning action and then you will hear the collapse sound and everyone "hits the floor" at once.*
Explain this to the children quite clearly, fairly slowly, and with a considerable amount of facial expression and use of hands.

19

GUIDED EXPERIENCE   *That was really good. Now actions are like words, we can use them in a different order and by altering the order we say something different. Go with a partner and together change those actions around into an order which suits you both.*

During the time that the children are working, move amongst them, watching, guiding, encouraging, letting alone, all the time trying to help the children to gain some form of satisfaction in either the process or the outcome of their work.

CLARIFY   1. *Everyone stop. Let me see you go through your piece of work once. Take your starting positions, and when you have finished hold your ending positions until everyone in the room has finished.*
Allow time for them to finish.
2. *Try that once again. See if you can improve on the ending, make sure that you do stay perfectly still in your final position.*

GUIDED EXPERIENCE   1. *Respond in action to these words as you hear them:*

gallop
roll
bounce
shiver
whirl
shrink
explode

2. *Everyone sit still for a minute and then go and change.*

NOTES TO THE TEACHER

1. The phrase *about* the room is used in preference to *around* the room. If the latter is used the children tend to circulate in one direction, only, rather like a group of "circus ponies".
2. When the children are asked to stop, following any moving activity, two short clear beats on the drum, either immediately preceding, or following, the sound of the voice, should be made. The children quickly associate the sound and the word, and in the following lessons there is seldom any need to use the voice command.
3. When children of any age are introduced to dance it is extremely important to keep them involved in a continuous rhythmical flow of movement. It is not sufficient to allow them to run and stop, once, and then shoot them on to something else. They require time to both relax and concentrate. This may sound contradictory but by relaxing is meant a loosening of mental tension and anxiety which often accompanies being involved in the unknown. Concentration on movement can only come about when the body is given time to repeat and absorb a movement without continuous interruption.

20

4. It is essential in this first lesson that the relationship between the teacher and the children is firmly established. The onus lies completely with the teacher. It is vital that the teacher understands exactly what *the children are feeling*. If the teacher is anxious, agitated, insecure, this will inevitably affect the class. The student teacher should do his utmost to control his very natural feelings of apprehension. The best possible way of doing this is to think about the children rather than about self.

5. When children are asked to perform before the class, this should be put in the manner of a request that is sincerely meant, not as a demand, or a right, on the part of the teacher. The teacher should, therefore, be very careful in his choice, and endeavour to recognize who will respond to this request. If in any doubt at all, he should have previously asked this child if he is willing to show his work. This should be done when all of the children are working and consequently there is no "loss of face" on either side.

6. It is important to establish, from the first lesson, that every piece of work has a definite starting and finishing position. In writing, a sentence begins with a capital letter and ends with a full stop. A movement sentence is constructed in the same way. This is important. Children find it very difficult to know when to stop moving. At the same time, they do not know what to do if they keep on moving. They repeat things in movement or just keep performing random actions. It is far better to aim for short, well articulated and composed pieces of work than for "sagas" which say little or nothing!

7. The lessons, particularly the first few, should be extremely demanding physically. Children—and boys in particular—at this age respond to sheer physical "work out": a little perspiration or a good sweat goes a long way towards helping them begin to accept this form of movement. However, as is stated in *Creative Dance for Boys*, "We wish to stress, however, that we do not subscribe to the view that only powerful action is masculine."

8. All lessons follow the pattern of guided experience; discovery, clarification, formulation, yet each contains its own variations. For example, this lesson ended with vigorous guided experience rather than with a final completed phrase of activity by the children. This is one possible way to end a movement lesson, and should be chosen in accordance with the needs of the moment.

Lesson 2

Material of the lesson / To review action words of the previous lesson and to work with new ones. To use action words accompanied by the music "Postillion".

21

Introduction

At the beginning of this lesson, review fairly quickly many of the words used in the previous lesson. This might be done in the following manner:

You are going to work on several different action words, some you already know, others will be new. Sometimes you will put sentences together, sometimes simply work on improving your skill with an action!

Spend about ten minutes guiding the children in the use of action words. These are not set down here because each case is unique. Teachers would be better advised to make their own selection from the list of action words found at the beginning of this chapter. The words should be carefully chosen. A travelling word such as run, skip gallop, hop can be followed by a word which does not necessarily travel. It might be jump, spin, bounce, or shiver. A vibratory word such as shake or quiver, might be followed by a soothing word such as spin, float, or hover. Words which need explosive energy can be followed by those requiring a continuous gentle energy. Sometimes these factors should be pointed out to the class but often the children should be guided into using their bodies in an ever increasing vocabulary of movement without being "fussed" by the transitions that are being asked of them.

Having worked with this material the lesson continues with the development of "Postillion".

GUIDED EXPERIENCE

1. *Find a space and stand facing me. With one jumping action make a 360° turn and end up facing me again. Do this several times and try going in both directions. See if you can make each jump higher than the previous one.*

2. *Now instead of staying on the spot to do this, make two or three consecutive turning jumps that help you to travel to another place. Do this several times.*

3. *When you come down to the floor from your jump don't get stuck there but immediately prepare yourself for the next turning jump.*

Leave the class to work on this activity for a few moments; you should move among them helping where necessary.

4. *Try only one turning jump but at the end of it make sure that you pause or balance. Do this several times until you can really control the pause.*

FORMULATE

Make a sentence of three turning jumps which take you travelling, and then pause.

22

Go with a partner and starting together, or apart, work on timing your turning jumps and pauses so that you travel one after the other. For example:

"A" goes with three turning jumps—pause
"B" goes with three turning jumps—pause
"A" goes with three turning jumps—pause
"B" goes with three turning jumps—pause.

    Decide what sort of meeting and parting situations will occur when you do this.

FORMULATE   *Listen to the first part of this music. You will be able to hear the turning and pausing repeated four times. Once you think you are ready to work with the music take your starting positions.*

Allow the class to work with the music twice, at the end of which time, almost all of the pairs should have satisfactorily evolved their own partner sequence. The music is, however, very fast and one or two children may find it hard to get the initial jumping turn started at the right time.

GUIDED EXPERIENCE   1. *Stand facing your partner and see which of you can jump the highest.*
2. *Fine! Now you have really got the feeling of pushing for height, can you retain this in a galloping action?*

Be careful that, as the children explore this idea, they do not lose some of the height of their earlier thrusting action the moment they start to travel.

3. *Stop travelling for a moment and make three very quick successive stamps onto the floor.*

FORMULATE   With each child working on his own.
Now make your sentence of action galloping—stamp, stamp, stamp.
At this point you give the children the length of the phrase on the drum.

GUIDED EXPERIENCE   *Sit and listen to the music all the way through. Now with your partner and, using the phrases of turning-jumps and pause, galloping and stamping, work with the music to create a meeting and parting dance.*

When the class has eventually finished working on this dance their phrasing may have become:

"A" turning jumps—pause
"B" turning jumps—pause
"A" turning jumps—pause
"B" turning jumps—pause

"A" and "B" gallop at the same time and then stamp at the same time
"A" and "B" repeat the gallop and stamp
"A" turning jumps—pause to finish
"B" turning jumps—pause to finish.

There will be some variations on this basic pattern and teachers using partner work with any of these grades could present some of the following problems:
1. Do you start together or apart?
2. Do you travel in the same direction or in opposite directions?
3. If you pause near to each other are you on the same level or at different levels?
4. How do you make it obvious that this is a dance for you and your partner and not simply you both taking turns at moving to the music?

NOTES TO THE TEACHER

1. The teacher will often use the terms "we" and "our" when giving the children direction. It is assumed that both the children and the teacher are involved in the lesson and that although their roles are different, in many respects they are also similar. Consequently, the terms "we" and "our" come more readily in speech than the term "you".
2. "Postillion" is also found as a lesson for a Grade 3 class in *Creative Dance in the First Three Grades*. There however the challenges are presented at a much simpler level. This is because "Postillion" is one of the ageless pieces of music which can be enjoyed by most children. It is an excellent example of how one idea can be presented to both Grade 3 and Grade 6 provided that the actual presentation and challenge is made suitable for the age of the children. A comparison between the lesson for Grade 3 and the lesson for Grade 6 will show this difference in presentation.
3. It is often possible at this age to give the children a movement problem at the end of one lesson which they can be *thinking* about for the following lesson. Here is an example: *Make a short composition in a group which uses some of the action words we have explored. You should try to include:*

a jumping word
a travelling word
a shivery word
a turning word
a sinking word

You may put the words in any order and if you wish, you may repeat one word several times, for example: jump, jump, jump.

24

Make your composition short.

Here are some suggestions for group work which might help you:

travel together
meet and part
meet and stay together
travel over and under each other
move all at the same time doing the same action
move all at the same time doing different actions
move one after the other in cannon form

In movement, working in a group is similar to working on a group project in art or being a member of an orchestra. In each case the culmination of your work is a group composition.

Lesson 3

Material of the lesson / To allow time for work on the movement problem and then to work to another piece of music, "The Clock".

Introduction

At the beginning of this lesson immediately set the children to work upon the movement problem. Within a space of three lessons the children will be capable of assuming considerably more responsibility for their own work. As they set about working on the movement problem, the teacher will be observing. It is necessary to look at the teacher's role in this particular situation.

Initially, the teacher's role is that of observer, not a static or passive observer but a mobile, empathetic one. The teacher communicates so much, in both stillness and movement, that this role, in itself, is worthy of care and study. The observant teacher will notice all or several of these reactions: children sometimes cease to work as she approaches because their ideas are still too new and they still feel too insecure to share them; as the teacher passes by they resume their work; children start to talk loudly and say, "let's do it again," making quite sure that the teacher hears. In other words, they have something to show, they feel good about it and they want both recognition and commendation. Later they want both recognition and help to improve. The children stop "horsing around" and try to look as if they were really getting on with the job all the time! Children look confused and glance at you for help without saying in words, "All the rest of the class seem to have got the idea but we are plain stuck!" There are other things which occur, but the foregoing are amongst the most common and it is essential that the teacher pauses, takes time to assess situations before acting. So often a teacher can interrupt too quickly when children are trying to create. She then stops the natural creative activity which was going on or which would have emerged, and forces her own conception of things upon the children.

After the first ten to fifteen minutes of the lesson, when the children have created, shared, viewed and discussed their work, the teacher can resume a more direct teaching role.

GUIDED EXPERIENCE 1. *Find a place and take a position near to the floor. Whenever you hear the drum tapped, very quickly make one short quick movement which starts you on a rising action.*
Repeat the sequence several times.
2. *This time make these short quick movements come very suddenly, one after another, in a stacatto way. At the same time you are rising. The effect you are trying to get is of a quick, jerky rising action. After several quick actions collapse to the floor again. Repeat this phrase through twice: Rising with sudden, stacatto actions—collapsing.*
The children should be given time to work on this idea but all the time a standard of performance should be demanded from them. They should be encouraged and challenged to make the action truly sudden and stacatto, to retain strength in the action and to know clearly which parts of their body are moving.

CLARIFY *Sit where you are for a moment. Listen to this phrase of the music: you will hear how it is the exact sound pattern of your movement pattern. Listen again and then take your starting position ready to move with the music.*
The children should work through this part of the dance several times until it is reasonably clear.

GUIDED EXPERIENCE 1. *The last phrase of your movement brings you, in a collapsing or sinking action, back to the floor from where you then have to explode into the air. Try this several times, by yourself, so that you feel your legs acting like a very strong spring which ejects you as high as possible.*
2. *Now add a galloping action to the spring so that you spring up and immediately start to gallop. Keep the gallop going for a phrase of eight which goes—and one, and two, and three, and four, —.*
At this point the teacher can immediately start to give the children audible help by beating out the rhythm on the drum.
3. *Pause for a moment and get your breath. Now try a strong backward turning action which takes you down to the floor. Try this turning action several times. Good! Now let's put the whole phrase together:*

26

Rising with stacatto action
Sinking
Rising again with stacatto action
Sinking
Explosive leap from the floor followed immediately by galloping
Freeze for a second and then a strong turning action back down to the floor.

FORMULATE   *Sit down where you are and listen to the music. You will hear the accompaniment to the phrases you have danced and then a complete repetition immediately comes again. When you are ready try to dance from beginning to end.*

The children should be immediately challenged to do this again, without spending time correcting details. After the second time, however, they might be asked:

Which part are you finding physically quite difficult?
Yes, Keith?
The part where you have to push up from the floor and immediately go into a gallop.
For that part you really need to be thinking ahead so that the music does not catch you by surprise. Any other part? Yes, Ann?
The part where you go down in a turn the first time and then have to immediately start the dance again.

27

Good, yes, that is another difficult part. All right let's try it again. The children should finish the lesson by going through "The Clock" once again.

NOTES TO THE TEACHER

1. When children start work in group work, they should be encouraged to start moving as quickly as possible. The maximum is **do**, don't talk. This holds good in almost all dance situations, even those with adults. Sitting and talking rather than doing tends to inhibit rather than enhance ideas.

2. At this point in the children's development some are still dependent upon the teacher to both provide the motivation and set the standard of work expected from them. Others are able to demand of themselves a good standard of work. The teacher is, therefore, commending, challenging, encouraging, and always reacting to the needs of the children as they display themselves in several ways.

3. When children first put any created dance to the music, they should be allowed to dance it through at least twice without being stopped. Mistakes which occur the first time are usually corrected the second time, quite automatically, by the children. Too much time spent on correction or niggling about details detracts from the spontaneity of the children's response and often makes them aware of and nervous of failure.

4. During the lesson, it is extremely interesting to watch the different approaches and attitudes to what is now really dance rather than movement experience. The following reactions often occurred: The boys enjoyed all the vigorous parts and delighted in a few grunts and groans. They were imaginative in their actions but certainly not in the least concerned with finesse or style. They tackled everything with a "football" approach, but were obviously gaining tremendous satisfaction. The girls on the other hand were concerned with precision and to a large extent with how they "looked" and the effect they were having on any observer. Even at this age, which was a Grade 6 group, it was fascinating to note the love of repetition of a favorite action. Don had achieved a superb turning jump and whenever the opportunity presented itself, there he was, performing this much liked action.

Lesson 4

Material of the lesson/ To review and consolidate previous learning.

This lesson should consist of a review of all the action words previously learned; although they should be presented in an original way using different combinations of words. For example; a sinking action might be introduced with the use of an interrupted, jerky flow of movement on the way down. A spin can be made very, very slowly with the emphasis on continuity of action. Group work on the movement problem and "The Clock" and "Postillion" should be repeated.

NOTES TO THE TEACHER

1. Children find tremendous satisfaction in both reviewing work previously developed and in re-dancing dances they have created in earlier lessons, and it is important that every so often they are given this opportunity. One Grade 4 class who had been creating a very short simple dance each lesson for six weeks had no problem in remembering these and dancing them one after the other. In fact they were most indignant, if, by any chance, the teacher happened to forget one. This is because the children and teacher had, together, created dances which were meaningful and appropriate for them.
2. It is important that the teacher decides how often children can change dances they have already created. This is a recurrent problem in children's work and it is important that the teacher think clearly about this.
3. The following two lessons are recorded in a different way because the normal format is too confusing to convey the excitement of exploring percussion with the children. These two lessons are recorded as they actually happened with a Grade 6 class.

Lessons 5 and 6

Material of the lessons / To give the children opportunities to explore the use of percussion to accompany their own actions in individual and partner compositions.

GUIDED EXPERIENCE

1. *Find a space. Listen to this phrase of drum sounds and think in terms of gallop—freeze—spin—sink (with quick, light, jerking actions)—explode.*
2. *This time as the sounds for the actions are created, start to move: gallop—freeze—spin—sink—explode!*

OBSERVATION

This was repeated three times and at the end of that time all of the children were able to complete the movement sentence without any hesitation.
3. *Each of the boys are to take a drum and a beater and work on accompanying yourself while you are doing that phrase of action. The girls come and listen to the sounds of the claves and the finger cymbals.*

29

What happened now was extremely interesting: the boys rushed for the case which carried the drums, obviously wanting to make sure that they would get one. From the way in which they had always been fascinated by the drum in previous lessons it had been apparent that once given one, they would need little further motivation to go ahead and use it. Now, not only were they able to hit it and make the desired noise, but they had an immediate and concrete problem upon which to work. No time was wasted on any activity which was not connected with the problem.

The girls, in the meantime, were clustered around the teacher listening to the type of sounds made by the claves and finger cymbals. They too were quickly moved onto a concrete problem, given below.

GUIDED EXPERIENCE

Go with a partner and one of you have a pair of claves and the other a pair of finger cymbals. Then think about how you might have a conversation in action. The claves speak. Perhaps they say, "I skip, skip, skip away from you and freeze."

The finger cymbals reply, "I turn very slowly towards you and sink."

Then the claves speak, followed again by the finger cymbals, then both instruments speak at once and end the conversation.

OBSERVATION From this moment, when all of the children were actively involved in working with an instrument, the remainder of this lesson and the following one became a time when the teacher followed the activities of the children and guided them by studying the situations that arose. Again the role of teacher had altered. She was actively following the lead of the children's interests all the time, watching that they did not, too often, start on a track which was going to end in frustration. It is absolutely essential that the teacher be willing to follow the children. From a deeper understanding and knowledge of both the children, themselves, and the movement problems they will encounter, she will be able to suggest ways and means for the children to develop their work.

Some of these resources will be noticed as we follow the class in the development of the work.

All of the children were now actively involved in working with the percussion. Gradually, some of the boys stopped working on the initial problem and began to experiment with other sounds and actions. Then discussion started to arise between boys. What would normally happen to cause this would be that in moving, two boys would bump into each other. From this often developed a "You wait until I've finished and then you can have the space." This soon became a shared activity in which *one did* and the *other watched*.

Other boys, on bumping, would immediately start a conversation which somehow always ended with them working together. Eventually, there were only three boys remaining who were working alone and obviously from choice. Others had paired up and the original problem had been entirely discarded. The teacher accepted this situation and continued to give guidance in whatever way seemed appropriate. Eventually, she drew all the class together and restated the idea of "conversation in action" to be worked upon by those who wished to do this. The children continued to work for approximately a further five minutes before the lesson was brought to a very informal close. From the moment that the children had been given the percussion to the end of the lesson, they had been given time to explore the instruments with complete freedom. The children's interest had ensured that this was extremely productive.

In the following lesson the children went immediately to the percussion and started work. Now they were given ten minutes in which to compose a phrase of actions accompanied by sound. The boys then watched the result of the girls' activity and the girls watched the boys'. During this time the following points on partner work were discussed:
1. Two people might start close together, or far apart, at the same level, at different levels.
2. Two people might move one after the other, both at the same time.
3. Two people might move away from, toward, around, or above, over, under each other.

After seeing each other's work, the immediate request from one of the more heavily built boys was, "Can we use those things?"—indicating the finger cymbals. The teacher's response was, "Those of you who wish to change instruments may do so." Practically everyone did want to. The pattern of exploration was then repeated with a new instrument.

In the following lessons the children frequently were given time to work with percussion but did not devote the whole of the time to percussion work.

NOTES TO THE TEACHER

The boys were given the drums and the girls were introduced to new instruments, the finger cymbals and the claves. This was done for the following reasons:

Most children enjoy playing an instrument but the method with which the instruments are introduced is very important.

These boys in Grade 6 were having their fifth and sixth lesson in creative dance. At times it was obvious that they still had anxieties caused by being the only boys in the school to be involved in this activity. Because of the nature of the instruments in size, shape and sound, the drums are a more masculine instrument than the claves or finger cymbals. To have asked the boys to start with the finer instruments could have been to invite them to be embarrassed. This they would probably have hidden by "clowning" in some form or another. As it was, they were given drums, a problem to solve and then virtually ignored. Even the attention of the teacher and girls was removed from the boys because the former were busily involved with something else. This gave the boys time to accommodate themselves to a new situation without being under pressure.

The girls in Grade 6 were a particularly gregarious group with strong attachments to particular friends. They enjoyed the prospect of working with a partner and in being able to talk to each other and work together. They, too, were able to overcome very easily any feeling of slight embarrassment which handling the instruments would give them. If anyone doubts this reaction to handling an instrument in the moving situation for the first time, it would be an excellent experience to go and actually do it and observe your own reactions.

Lesson 7

Material of the lesson / An experiment in group work using the music "The Spinning Song" by Kullak.

GUIDED EXPERIENCE

1. *Everyone find a partner and take up a position in which you are standing face to face. When the drum is beaten once, make a swift darting action to one side of your partner. Now try it to the other side.*
Experiment for a few minutes with this idea.
Dart to one side.
Dart to the other side.
Swiftly run a short distance away from and then back towards your partner.
The children should be given time to practice this. If you are in doubt as to the activity, place your hands palm to palm. Now move the right hand swiftly to the right and the left hand to the left. Take them apart and bring them back together, swiftly. This is the effect in miniature.

FORMULATE

Try to put together this sentence of action with your partner:
Dart to one side,
Dart to the other side,
Run . . . .
Repeat this action sentence four times altogether.

33

The children should try this phrase through several times without being too concerned with the rhythm. Then the teacher should beat out the rhythm of the phrase on the drum. (See Notes to the Teacher 4). This is repeated several times until the children are familiar with the phrasing and have worked out how they can best organize their own actions into a smooth continuous flow.

GUIDED EXPERIENCE

1. *Stay away from your partner and practice four very high leaping actions followed by a slow turning action. As you turn quite deliberately look at all four corners of the room.*
2. *Now work out how you can make your phrase:*
Leap, leap, leap, leap
Turn, turn, turn, turn
Leap, leap, leap, leap
Turn, turn, turn, turn
The class should be given time to work out this phrasing.

FORMULATE

1. *Sit and listen for the way the actions and phrasing you have been using fit into the first part of the music:*
Dart to one side
Dart to the other side
Run . . . .
Repeat 4 times
Leap, leap, leap, leap
Turn, turn, turn, turn
Repeat twice
2. *Everyone up and try this right the way through twice with the music.*

GUIDED EXPERIENCE

1. *During the last turning action which you have just performed you see your partner again and approach him. Try to join together, turning and approaching to meet your partner.*
2. *When you meet your partner decide how you will confront each other.*
3. *Facing each other bring about the idea of conflict or opposition which eventually causes you to break away from one another.*

CLARIFY

Work on this sequence: turning—seeing your partner—approaching —opposing—parting.
Suggestions which will help the children to clarify this part of the work might be:
How do you approach your partner? Are you facing him or moving backwards?
What is your action as you approach? Is it creeping, rolling, strong stepping?

34

Is the pathway on the floor directly towards your partner or do you try to move around to meet him?

When you confront each other are you at the same level or different ones?

Which part of your body is important when you oppose each other? Is it your hands, or your hips, or your legs?

Can you build up sufficient tension in your confrontation to make it necessary for you to break away from each other?

FORMULATE *Work through with the music from the beginning, darting—running —leaping—turning—approaching—confronting—leaving. Remember the parts which have to be repeated.*
Work through this part with the children more than once.

GUIDED EXPERIENCE *1. The entire first part of the music repeats itself until the end. As you finally break away from your partner the momentum makes you travel and you meet a different partner. Repeat the first part of the dance.*
2. Let's practice breaking away and finding a new partner. Go with your first partner and when you hear the drum beats, break away and whirl to meet someone else.
It may be necessary to continue repeating the sequence until the children have each found a new partner. Once they have found the new partner they do not need to repeat the earlier experiences but can complete the dance.

FORMULATE *Take your starting position with your first partner and be ready to go through the whole dance.*
Having worked through the dance as individuals, with some partner relationship, the children were given the following problem.

GUIDED EXPERIENCE *See if using this framework of the dance you can create a group dance which in some ways tells of a dramatic event. Choose your own group and if you wish to you can relate to another group.*

OBSERVATION The following is a recorded observation of how the children developed the group work.

Two groups are searching for each other and they dodge to one side and then another, in their attempt to find each other. They perform this dodging in a small way, using little space. They then run to another spot and look again using the same dodging action. Having done this four times, and still not being able to see each other, they start to leap high in the air. Using these leaps they hope to be better able to see each other. They leap four times and, not seeing each other, they make a turning action in which they continue searching. They repeat both the leaps and the turns. This time they see and start to approach each other. When they meet the opposing group they suddenly turn and, using very strong, powerful pressing action, they appear to battle. In this instance, they do not touch each other, but alternately rise and sink as one presses down and then the other presses up. They do not resolve this fight and so break away and commence the whole dance sequence again, from the beginning. The dance evolves in the same way, until the very end, when they suddenly turn, confront each other and stop.

1. Whenever a specific piece of music is mentioned as appropriate for certain actions and a formulated dance, this dance will have been created by the teacher. Everyone should feel free to interpret the music in their own way and create dances which are appropriate to the needs of their own class. However, the dance as set down in this lesson may be of value to teachers who require more guidance in this aspect.

2. This dance is fairly directed in its structure but, even within that, each child was performing the dance with his own variation of style and adding his own touches which made it come alive for him.

3. It must be understood that creative dance is always a balance between freedom to create and conformation to a discipline. Complete freedom is chaos.

4. Whenever the teacher is working with pre-selected music she should have listened to it a sufficient number of times prior to teaching in order to be able to beat out the general phrasing of the music for the children. When they have worked through the guided experiences with a drum accompaniment they can then readily work with the music.

Lesson 8

Material of the lesson / To use "The Eagle" by Alfred, Lord Tennyson as a stimulus for a group dance.

GUIDED EXPERIENCE   *Everyone come over here to the center of the room and sit down for a moment to listen to this poem.*

THE EAGLE

He clasps the crag with crooked hands;
Close to the sun in lonely lands,
Ring'd with the azure world, he stands.

The wrinkled sea beneath him crawls;
He watches from his mountain walls,
And like a thunderbolt he falls.

Alfred, Lord Tennyson

DISCUSSION   *This eagle is powerful, and if we were depicting his strength and power in actions we would probably use leaping, turning, pausing with a very strong feeling in the body, perhaps hovering and certainly swooping.*

How would you imagine the sun would be depicted? Yes, circling, turning, rising, sinking.

Would the sun's action have the same power as the eagle's? Yes, they might have but would also be slower and more continuous.

The sea—what kind of action for that? Shivering, tumbling, turning again, rising.

And how about the wall? Try taking very strong wide or angular shapes and move them with jumps and with jerky actions.

GUIDED EXPERIENCE *1. Which of you wish to work on the wall and who wants to work on the eagle?*

OBSERVATION The boys elected to have about six or seven in the wall and the others were to work on being individual eagles!

2. Which of you wish to work upon the sun and the sea?

The girls divided into groups of three for the sun and six or seven for the sea. There were therefore about six eagles, one wall, one sea, and two suns—a situation which bothered neither the teacher nor the children, though it might well disturb the maker of the universe! The children then selected percussion for their groups. Drums for the wall; finger cymbals for the sun; tambourine for the sea.

NOTES TO THE TEACHER

1. One can be continually astounded by children and made to realize how, too often, we do not give them sufficient scope for their own powers of invention. In this lesson the teacher became almost superfluous. As had happened with the percussion, the children were completely motivated into activity.

2. The group who seemed to be encountering the greatest difficulty was the sea, but this was not insurmountable.

3. The girls developed a turning motif which carried the sun from one place to another as it rapidly rose and set: the sound of the finger cymbals was particularly effective. Eagles were busy leaping, swooping and hovering and the occasional "Caw, Caw" was heard. The wall presented a formidable line as it heaved itself "zombie-like" across the gym to the accompanying "bang-bang-bang". The sea was being turbulent in more than one way. The girls were having social rather than movement problems which were not entirely resolved.

4. After about fifteen minutes, the children's experimentations were stopped and the scene set by grouping them in certain spatial locations. These groupings were dependent upon the space available and the needs of the poem. For example, initially the wall would not want to be very close to the sun. Neither should the eagles be grouped together. The teacher should be very aware of the spacing of the groups because this will effect the total outcome of the group dance. Once the groupings have been placed, the final drawing together of all the ideas can begin.

38

The children now move to the accompaniment of the spoken word: Below the poem is re-written with the children's actions at the side:

"The Eagle"	Very still, in group, or individual starting positions
He clasps the crag with crooked hands;	Eagles leap, swoop, turn and travel;
Close to the sun in lonely lands,	Eagles freeze near to sun and sun commences rising and turning,
Ring'd by the azure world, he stands.	Eagles move slightly and then again start to travel. Sun has stopped moving.
The wrinkled sea beneath him crawls;	The eagle now pauses near to the sea and the sea starts to move;
He watches from his mountain walls,	Sea stops moving and eagle travels to wall. Wall starts to move and continues moving until they hear words . . . ,
And like a thunderbolt he falls.	Wall ceases to move, but eagles, sea and sun all move for a few seconds and then everything stops.

Having explained the general idea to the class, they tried the whole thing twice accompanying the words with their actions.

NOTES TO THE TEACHER

1. "The Eagle" is so delightfully placed and illustrated in the *Oxford Book of Poetry for Children,* compiled by Edward Blishen and illustrated by Brian Wildsworth, that the most natural and exciting way to interest the children in this verse is, simply, to take the book along with you to the movement lesson and show it to the class at the beginning of the lesson.
2. This approach should only be used when verse, story or legend is sufficiently brief to allow a few minutes for it to be read at the beginning of the lesson.
3. Some people might feel that this brief treatment of the verse is doing it an injustice. This is not intended, and in a later lesson in the classroom the whole beauty of the verse would be fully explored.
4. It would also be possible to explore the verse before the movement lesson. Whichever way it is presented, the presentation of the verse for the first time and the movement lesson should be suffi-

ciently close to each other for the children to retain the feeling, the mood and the excitement of the poem.

5. The teacher has to be constantly on the alert for the children's point of no return in any one lesson. This will vary but there always comes a point when to persist with a thing will destroy it. The reason for reaching this point is not always apparent and seldom is it the same twice over. The teacher has to be sensitive to its happening and at that point, in some way, change the situation for the children. Later they can return to the original work with renewed interest. (Although sometimes a thing is dead and buried and should not be resurrected.)

CONCLUSION

These eight lessons were worked with a Grade 6 class being introduced to creative dance for the first time. In a school with an established dance program the work with action words would normally have been covered in the earlier grades. However the presentation in those grades would have been at a simpler level and the rate of learning would have been far slower. Teachers who have a class in Grades 5 and 6 with previous dance experience will be able to use these ideas but should make further adjustments to the lessons. They should place more emphasis upon:

a) the dynamics present in each action word,

b) the subtle distinction between similar actions, for example, whirl, twirl, shiver, shake,

c) greater fluency and understanding of transitions between words,

d) an increase in movement of different body parts to leading emphasis actions,

e) a deeper control and understanding of the body shape both in moving and stillness.

REFERENCE

Carroll, Jean and Perter Lofthouse. *Creative Dance for Boys.* London: Macdonald and Evans, 1969.

Verse Used in Lesson 8
"The Eagle" by Alfred, Lord Tennyson. Blishen, Edward and Brian Wildsworth. *Oxford Book of Poetry for Children* London: Oxford University Press, 1963.

MUSIC REFERENCES

Lesson 2: "Postillion" by Godard. Volume III, *Basic Rhythms Program for Primary Grades.*

Lesson 3: "The Clock" by Kullak. Volume III, *Basic Rhythms Program for Primary Grades.*

Lesson 7: "Spinning Song" by Kullak. Volume II, *Basic Rhythms Program for Primary Grades.*

2

EFFORT

A group of children who had been introduced to creative dance were using action words. As they explored the action of spinning, most were working at a fairly moderate speed. Each one was enjoying, obviously, a different aspect of the movement sensation. Some were enjoying the feeling of having their arms widespread as they spun around, some were undulating and enjoying the moments of off-balance. Nikki was exploring her spin with such a feeling of "lingering" and "delicacy" that the action had become of far less importance to her than these two other movement sensations.

This slipping into unselfconscious exploration and enjoyment of the quality of the action is an essential stage in children's dance. As they are helped to become aware of the qualitative sensation of actions they are learning the art and experience of using "texture". As Nikki continued to move, it became apparent that she had a natural love of the feeling of lightness and sustainment. Seldom was the work of her own choosing shot through with any strong, powerful, sudden actions.

The teacher, in order to understand the importance of "texture" or quality in children's actions, has to understand how this element is not only present in movement but can play a vital part in children's movement education.

To return to Nikki: imagine for a moment that all her actions are coloured predominately with two elements of movement: A love of sustained lingering and an enjoyment of gentleness, delicacy and lightness. This is a part of Nikki, as important and unique to her as the colour of her eyes and hair. Although these movement colours predominate, she will need others if she is going to express herself in different ways. To expose her to other qualities and textures of movement will enrich her range and the store of movement qualities from which she can then discover other forms of expression.

This in fact is what working with dynamics, quality or effort means. It is an enrichment and widening of the child's qualitative movement that leads to greater expression in action.

For each child the "tipping over" into absorption with quality rather than action will come at different times and to different degrees. It is impossible to state that, at a given moment, the class should be ready to learn about this qualitative aspect of movement. The teacher however needs to be aware that, gradually, this will happen and to be ready with her own knowledge and understanding of movement content to go with the children into this new area of dance experience.

What are these qualitative movement sensations which the children will start to explore as they are using action words?

THE MOVEMENT SENSATION OF TIME

This sensation has two extreme ends: one of rapidity, haste, urgency, immediacy, i.e., suddenness; and one of lingering and never-ending, i.e., sustainment. Between the ends of the continuum come the sensations of time which fall into neither of these two categories: sudden and sustained.

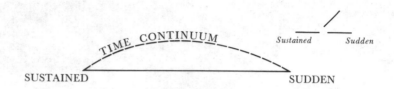

THE MOVEMENT SENSATION OF ENERGY

This sensation has two extreme ends: one of strength and power, i.e., firmness; and one of delicacy and lightness, i.e., finetouch. Between the ends of this continuum come the sensations of energy which fall into neither of these two categories: firm and finetouch.

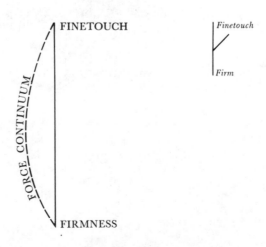

THE MOVEMENT SENSATION OF SPACE

This sensation has two extreme ends: the one where the sensation is of directness, completely undeviating, focused beyond any intention of change, i.e., directness; and the other of plasticity, wandering and meandering, i.e., flexibility. Between the two ends of this continuum come the sensations of space which fall into neither of these categories: direct and flexible.

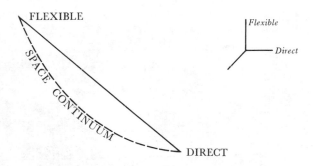

These three groupings: sudden-sustained, firm-finetouch, direct-flexible, constitute the time, weight, space, motion factors together known as "complete effort". It is the effort, within the action words, which gives the colour, texture or quality to the action. Children's dance experience will be enriched by exploring these movement sensations.

When exploring these movement sensations it is extremely important to notice vocabulary. The term for the motion factors will often be described in imaginative, colourful ways in order to help the children achieve the required sensation. "Finetouch" may be described as light, delicate, gentle; and "suddenness" as quick, brisk, urgent, etc. The teacher should be aware that although descriptive words may be used in the following lessons they refer back to the correct terms for the motion factors of time, weight and space.

Knowing this gives the teacher the opportunity of structuring lessons and experiences which now emphasize quality of movement.

LESSONS ABOUT THE TEXTURE OF TIME AND ENERGY

The following lessons are not given for a specific grade for these reasons. It is assumed that the material in Chapter 1 will form the introductory work for dance. Once the introductory work has been

accomplished children will explore "effort" at different levels of understanding and ability. One Grade 4 class may enjoy the work with effort symbols at a simple level. A Grade 6 class may continue to work in some depth with the ideas of effort symbols. By freeing the lessons from a specific indication of grade level the teacher is given greater opportunity to adapt and adjust the material to the needs of her class. The material itself is presented to give ideas on how to *introduce* "effort" to children and the lesson plans need not be taught sequentially.

Lesson 1
Material of the lesson / To develop an awareness of firmness and finetouch.

GUIDED EXPERIENCE

1. *Everyone find a partner and come and sit down. What would happen if you and your partner were working on a see-saw or a teeter-totter?*
From this question will come several suggestions, but the principle which should be drawn out is the one of action and reaction.
2. *Go away and work on the idea that one of you makes a strong downward action which causes your partner to shoot into the air.*
Allow the children time to experiment freely with this idea.

DISCOVER

Come and sit down again and let's discuss what happened.
1. *Those of you who were making the strong actions did you use your force or energy in a downward or upward direction?*
Yes, downward.
2. *Before you make a strong downward action did you feel yourself take a breath and move slightly in an upward direction?*
You will find that the children once having had their attention drawn to this fact will realize that this is what did happen.
3. *Those of you who were shooting upwards, did you find that before you "shot up" you did in fact sink very slightly?*
Again the children will realize that this is what had happened. From these three questions which have grown out of the children's practical experience it is a simple step to lead them into exploring the two opposite sensations of firmness and finetouch.

GUIDED EXPERIENCE

Find a space and practice different kinds of strong, sudden actions, perhaps a jump, stamp, turn, or spreading action. Allow the children several minutes to work on this idea.
Now instead of just stopping in between each action, make this a definite pausing action which is very important because it is light in quality. Perhaps a strong inward turn followed by a very light spreading.
Allow the children time to explore this idea—giving help whenever it is needed.

47

DISCOVER   1. *Do your strong actions always have to be sudden or can they in fact be lingering and sustained?*
2. *Do your light actions always have to be lingering or can they be sudden?*
How the children discover this can be left to practice, observation, or question and answer situations. Each teacher must use the most effective method for her children. However, once this idea has been examined by the children, they should be involved in moving again.

FORMULATE   1. *Decide upon a sentence of movement in which you show the movement sensation of strength and lightness through your actions.*
2. *Work this through once or twice until it is very clear to you the point when you change from one to the other.*

NOTES TO THE TEACHER

1. In order to convey any idea to children, the teacher should use every expressive medium possible—words, sounds, pictures, voice. In this lesson the hands, in particular, can be used to convey the qualities of strength and lightness to the children. For example, at the moment when the children are exploring the idea of emphasizing "the pause" with lightness.
2. A lesson plan such as this sounds as dry as dust. It isn't. The imaginative and involved teacher who captures the essence of quality in movements for the children and then, sharing it with them, involves them in their own discoveries, will be excited and stimulated by the results.

Lesson 2

Material of the lesson / To continue exploring the idea of firmness and finetouch/sudden and sustained quality in movement.

GUIDED EXPERIENCE   1. *Everyone find a place and crumple up on the floor!*
2. *Really feel floppy, relaxed and crumpled. Now listen to the drum beat and, as you hear the sound, gradually stiffen every muscle until you are firm and rock-like.*
3. *Relax. Crumple again.*
Repeat this phrasing several times, without any interruptions.
4. *Now, instead of relaxing between each held shape, make a strong, slow action or actions before you freeze again.*
This action may take the children from one place to another before they resume their frozen shapes.

DISCOVER   *How else can you arrive in any frozen shape without getting there with a powerful, slow action?*

48

As the children start to show different ways of achieving this, let them watch ways which bring out:
a) light, lingering, sustained actions
b) strong, sudden actions
c) light, sudden actions.
Help them to both recognize and verbalize what they see.

CLARIFY   *You have been using actions which are either:*

firm/sudden – strong/quick – like "explode"
firm/sustained – strong/slow – like "press"
finetouch/sudden – light/quick – like "shiver"
finetouch/sustained – light/slow – like "drift"

Form a group of three or four. Decide which movement qualities you would bring out in describing one of the following:
a wall (For example, Is it strong and powerful? Would it move slowly or quickly?)
a rock
a cloud
boiling water
a bulldozer
"thinking things out"
"black and white".
Once you have decided, create a short movement sequence which shows your ideas.
Here are listed some of the ideas which might be presented to children, these can be altered to suit the needs of each individual class. The teacher may also be required to help some groups, while others will prefer to be completely independent.

FORMULATE   *Once you have practiced a few of your ideas make a very short dance or movement sequence which shows particularly the quality of movement in your idea.*

NOTES TO THE TEACHER

1. The word "crumple" is used instead of lie because it will create more asymmetric shapes and the children will find it easier to move again. (When "lie on the floor" is used the children usually choose flat symmetrical shapes which have less potential for movement.)
2. When the children are working from a low position walk amongst them as you drum, so retaining a communication with them.
3. The lesson gives the children considerable scope for either achieving some very creative work or floundering and achieving little. There is no middle way. However, by sometimes allowing the possibility of "floundering" we can assess the levels of creativity to

which children aspire as well as achieve. Too often we underestimate the work of which they are capable.

It is absolutely vital, in all the work with the texture or quality of movement, that teachers realize the children do not have to be dancing about stories, ideas, moods, events or even action words. Dancing with the movement ideas of strong, light, sudden, sustained, direct, flexible, free and bound movements is sufficient.

Lesson 3

Material of the lesson / To become familiar with symbols for firmness and finetouch and to read these symbols to create a dance phrase.

GUIDED EXPERIENCE

1. *You all know that for music it is possible to write down symbols which mean certain musical terms. It is also possible to write down symbols for movement. One of the systems used for recording movement is known as "Labanotation". Today we will write down and then dance to the symbols for firmness (strong actions) and finetouch (light actions).*
This symbol ╱ means that we are going to move. When we add ⌠ the second symbol underneath it we are going to move and make a very strong action.
2. *Everyone get up and find a space and make three strong actions one after the other.*
Once the children have worked with these three strong
actions, record it on the board ⌠ ⌠ ⌠
3. *Now try making two strong actions with only a hand.*
Write this on the board ⌠ hand ⌠ hand
4. *Come back to the board a minute. There is another symbol and this ⌡ means light or finetouch. The difference in these symbols is that the strong one is beneath this sign ╱ , the light one is above this sign.*
5. *See if you can work this out with five whole actions.* ⌡ ⌠ ⌡ ⌠ ⌠
For the remainder of this lesson the children can be given very simple problems to solve. Some of the possible ones are listed below:
a) *Make a sentence using three isolated body parts, one after the other.*

b) *Make a ⌠ jump.*

c) *Make a ⌡ turn.*

d) *Go with a partner and in action have a conversation which goes:* ⌠ ⌠ ⌠ ⌡ ⌡ *You may either both speak (move) at once or one after the other.*

50

In this lesson and in the following ones, once the children have become familiar with the symbols, they can be set many short simple movement problems to solve. Within the problems set there should be some degree of choice. It is also possible for the children to create their own strong and light phrases of action and then record what they have done.

Lesson 4

Material of the lesson / To become familiar with the symbols for sudden and sustained action.

GUIDED EXPERIENCE

1. *Everyone walk about the room and respond in action to whatever you hear.*
The teacher should then say certain things which the children both enjoy and respond to immediately; some of these are:
Hit the deck!
Run for your life!
Hide!
Caught you!

These can be repeated several times and between each the children are momentarily walking.
2. *Choose anyone of those ideas and really bring out the suddenness in the action.*
Allow time for the exploration of this idea.
3. *It is possible to write a symbol which means a sudden action of the whole body or a sudden action of parts of the body. First write in the sign for action* ╱ *and then below and to the right put a horizontal line* ╱_ .

DISCOVER

Try the following ideas:
a) ╱_ ╱_ ╱_   *actions of the whole body.*

b) ╱_   *jump,*

c) ╱_ *collapse.*

Once the children have explored how to work all of the movements, those who are ready can be challenged to complete a whole phrase consisting of a, b, and c.

GUIDED EXPERIENCE

1. *Listen to the sound of the cymbal. For as long as you hear it, make one continuous action, for example, a turn, rising, a step, a leap. Complete only one action to the whole length of the phrase.*
2. *Try another action, and this time the sound will be even longer in duration. You will have to move even more slowly.*

51

3. *Here is the symbol for a sustained action* _′ . *Notice that the horizontal stroke is now "lagging behind" the action sign.*

DISCOVER *Using one whole action for each symbol, work through these phrases:*

a) _′_′ ′_′_

b) _′_′_′ ′_

c) ′_ _′_′ ′_

d) ′_ _′_′_′

Once the children have had time to work through one or all of these problems set the further challenge.

FORMULATE *Find a partner and show him one of those phrases. See if he can guess which one it is you are doing.*

NOTES TO THE TEACHER

1. When commencing the work on sustained action with the cymbal, make the first two sounds fairly short, then gradually extend the length of the sound. In this way you will increase the challenge. All the time insist that only one action may be performed.

2. Although a sustained leap is very difficult to do, the children can capture the quality of the lifting action involved in leaping.

Once the children have acquired the art of reading the time and energy symbols (known as the time/weight symbols) the teacher and children can spend several lessons interpreting problems which the teacher sets, and those which the children set for each other.

Lesson 5

Material of the lesson / To use symbols to explore the four time/energy factors of movement.

GUIDED EXPERIENCE *You now know the different symbols for strong, light, sudden, sustained actions and you also know that often an action contains two of these factors. For example, it might be a strong and sudden leap that you are performing.*

DISCOVER *Go with a partner and using whole body actions show the meaning of the following symbols:*

a) ⌊_   c) _⌊

b) −⌠   d) ⌠−

It will take the children several minutes to work out these symbols and some children may not succeed in completing all four. However,

52

as they will be meeting these symbols many times, it is not necessary to wait until every single child in the class can easily read them.

GUIDED EXPERIENCE

1. *Go into groups of five and decide which of the four symbols you will choose to work with.*
2. *Select three whole body actions that you will perform with that particular quality.*
Allow time for working with this problem.

DISCOVER

How can you make the stillness, at both the beginning and the end of your three actions, also depict the quality you have chosen?

FORMULATE

Make your complete phrase of:
stillness
action a
action b
action c
stillness
and then repeat the whole phrase once again.

NOTES TO THE TEACHER

1. The outline of this lesson is quite brief because the children will need a considerable amount of time to solve the problems.
2. The teacher's guidance and observation is of paramount importance in lessons where the children are all solving problems at a different rate and depth.

The last three lessons have indicated one possible way of working with children on the quality or texture of movement. These lessons have also introduced the children to the fact that movement can be notated.

The following lessons will show how percussion, words, and music can also help to enrich the quality of children's movements. Two lessons will be devoted to the ways percussion instruments affect qualitative movement. Two more will be devoted to words and two to music. Again these lessons are sample lessons of approaches which have been used and found successful. They should, however, be freely interpreted and adapted to meet the needs of different groups and situations.

> The teacher should encourage the child to participate fully in these four incomplete effort qualities and repeat them over several months in different ways, so that the child can then recognize the sensation of each and learn to enjoy those which he found unfamiliar to start with. Play and learning situations should be provided in a variety of ways, including imitation and partner work.[1]

[1]Valerie Dunlop Preston, *A Handbook for Modern Educational Dance* (London: MacDonald and Evans Ltd., 1963).

53

MUSIC

The following two lessons use music as an accompaniment to the quality of actions. Often, when music which is distinctive in time and energy qualities is used, it very naturally, suggests mood, story or character. It is, however, extremely important to give the children the opportunity of working with music which remains abstract in character. In this way the children can explore more fully the movement quality, without being unduly influenced by the mood of the music. Certain pieces of music are particularly appropriate for this. The following come from the series of records *Modern Dance* composed by Ada Heynssen.

Lesson 6

Material of the lesson / To explore the use of strong and sudden actions of the whole body and body parts. To use these actions to the accompaniment of "Slashing and Punching" composed by Ada Heynssen, on *Modern Dance Record Number I*.

GUIDED EXPERIENCE
1. Find a space and stand firmly with your feet apart and your right arm lifted back to the right side of your head.
2. When you hear the drum beat make a strong "chopping" action down and across your body and immediately take the arm back again. You should lead with the side of the hand rather than the palm.
3. Repeat this rhythmically several times, both on the right side and the left side of the body.

DISCOVER
Now, instead of keeping the action going in one place only, try making that strong sudden action at different levels and in different places around your body.
Allow time for this and, if it will help the children's understanding, use some demonstration and observation. The action is very similar to a chopping action but the whole body is involved.

GUIDED EXPERIENCE
1. Sit and listen to this phrase of music. You will hear a phrase of four strong sudden actions immediately followed by three strong sudden actions.
2. The music may be even shorter and stronger than your actions were. Try now and fit an action into each piece of the phrase.
Repeat this experience with the music several times.

CLARIFY
Decide exactly how you are going to use these seven strong sudden actions. Each time be able to repeat the whole seven exactly the same as before.

GUIDED EXPERIENCE
1. Clench a hand until you have made a very firm fist. Make several strong "punching" actions with your fist in many places around your body trying at the same time to keep your whole body tensed and firm.
2. Sometimes let the action come across your body, sometimes let it move away from your body in different directions.
Once the children have explored this aspect fully:
3. Rest for a moment and listen to the second phrase of the music. This has eight actions in it.

DISCOVER
Repeat the first seven strong actions, which you did originally; now discover how you are going to use the next eight actions. Remember that these new actions are distinguished by a clenched fist.
Allow time for exploration and clarification.

GUIDED EXPERIENCE
Stop working. Now try, instead, to capture a strong, sudden, explosive quality in an action. All the energy should burst outwards from the center of you.
At this point the children are likely to explore leaping and turning actions. This should be encouraged as it will give them an opportunity of feeling the sensation in the strong, sudden airborne action.

DISCOVER
Work on three *explosive, outward-going actions. Make sure that you know exactly how you are going to recover between each one.*

GUIDED EXPERIENCE
1. Sit and listen to the whole piece of music and you will hear:

First Phrase	ƒ ƒ ƒ ƒ ƒ ƒ	*chopping action*
Second Phrase	ƒ ƒ ƒ ƒ ƒ ƒ ƒ ƒ	*punching action*
Third Phrase	ƒ ƒ ƒ	*three explosive leaps.*

2. Try working with the music to find out how you can manage the change between the chopping actions, the punching actions, and the explosive actions.

FORMULATE
Once the class has had time to work with the music to capture its phrasing and quality in their actions, they should be encouraged to formulate and repeat their work.

NOTES TO THE TEACHER

1. At the beginning of the lesson, it is far better for the teacher to demonstrate, immediately, the required action, rather than try to arrive at it verbally.
2. Children, particularly girls, often try to make strong sudden actions with their arms without having any tension in the rest of their body. Consequently, it is very difficult for them to really produce any sensation of strength.

55

Lesson 7

Material of the lesson / To explore the use of light sustained actions accompanied by the music "Gliding and Floating" from *Modern Dance Record Number I,* composed and played by Ada Heynssen.

GUIDED EXPERIENCE

1. *Everyone find a space and sit and listen to this piece of music. As you listen, think about the quality of the music, and try to describe it to yourself.*

Suggested adjectives to look for: light; gentle; delicate; waving; sad; melancholy; curving.

After the music stops continue with the following:

2. *When you are doing the next action think of the word you might be using. From where you are sitting, reach forward and put one hand very lightly on the floor. Touch the floor with the finger tips only.*

3. *Very gently and slowly lift that hand, trace a pattern in the air and then very lightly put your hand down in another place.*

Allow the children time to repeat this activity several times; if the sound of a cymbal ringing would help the children, use this as an accompaniment. Also give the children an opportunity to use the other hand.

4. *As you are repeating your action, sometimes increase its size. Let yourself completely change your position. Perhaps you change from sitting to kneeling, to standing, to lying.*

DISCOVER

1. *Listen to the first phrase of the music again. As you listen, see if you hear the beginning and end of each action.*

2. *Find out how your actions are clearly phrased with the music. You will find that sometimes the action is quite short; sometimes it goes on for a longer time; sometimes it even comes in waves.*

When the children have explored this idea sufficiently, give a short time to observation. Note the following things: it is necessary to keep a certain amount of muscular tension in the body throughout all the actions (even when the hands predominate). Often, it is fairly easy to maintain lightness when the action is rising but much more difficult to maintain when the action is sinking. Light, finetouch, sustained actions can be led by several parts of the hands—knuckles, finger tips, palms, sides—and also by other parts of the body, such as head, knees, feet, elbows.

Actions which may occur are rising, sinking, turning, whirling, settling.

GUIDED EXPERIENCE

1. *Find a place; try to make a jumping action in which you feel, for a second, that you actually hover, or suspend in the air.*

2. *As you start your push off from the floor really breathe in. The*

air you take into your lungs will make you feel lighter in the air.
3. Try several jumps. Don't make them so high that you have to strain and tense up in the air.

CLARIFY   *Join together several of these light jumps all the time keeping the buoyancy and feeling of being airborne.*
Allow time for this to happen.

GUIDED EXPERIENCE   1. *Now try running for a very short distance; as you run, your feet should hardly touch the floor.*
2. *When you pause, before you run, feel the really strong tension that you need in your leg muscles. This helps you stay "on top" of the floor instead of sinking heavily into it.*
Again give the children time to work at this problem.

FORMULATE   *Sit and listen once again to the music, this time all the way through. As you listen, be deciding how you will design your dance. Use any of the ideas which you have been practising in this lesson: Touching the floor, rising, sinking, whirling, settling, jumping. Remember that the most important aspect is the quality of lightness and sustainment. Think again of the word which describes your dance.*

Give the children the opportunity to formulate their ideas and then, if possible, have half the class perform at one time, in order that the children can see the different interpretations which have occurred.

NOTES TO THE TEACHER

1. This lesson began with the children listening to the music in order to help them towards capturing both the mood and the quality of the movement which is to follow. This might not be the right way to start with a class. They may need to be gradually led from strong vigorous activity to the point where it is possible to work with this sustained, light, delicate quality of movement. The beginning experiences in every lesson will set the right tone and atmosphere for what is to follow. In lessons where the stress is particularly on quality, the teacher must endeavour to find the right way towards this learning experience.

2. In the second part of this lesson, there is a definite change in the way the children are guided towards experiencing light sustained quality in action. This has been done because it is extremely exhausting, both physically and mentally, to stay with one quality for a long time.

WORDS

Boys, in particular, enjoy an element of the dramatic and humorous in their movements. Practically everyone has witnessed the "dramatic death" of the wounded gangster as he clutches somewhere around the heart region and sinks groaning to the ground! Follow children closely in their natural activities and they will often lead you to the way to approach their movement lessons; a way that is more natural and right than an adult could conceive.

This lesson is based on children's delight in any form of hunt, fight or search; but it is so developed that the words are used only as motivators. Movement quality is of prime importance rather than the sequence in a story.

58

Lesson 8

Material of the lesson / To explore the words: flee, stalk, capture, release, to help bring out specific time/energy quality in action.

GUIDED EXPERIENCE *Everyone find a place and when you hear the drum beats start running and freezing.*
Repeat several times, changing the length of the phrases.

DISCOVER *Think of the word "flee" and show that instead of simply running that your action has in it the intent to flee.*
Leave the children with this problem for a short time. Then, through observation and discussion, draw their attention to what you have seen. Some children will have made very rapid changes in their floor pattern.

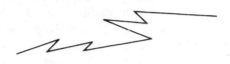

Some will have really emphasized the feeling and action of a pause with a very sudden spurt at the beginning of their run. Some will have emphasized the head, in short, sharp, almost furtive turning actions as they look around before "fleeing". If your children have responded simply with a fast run, draw their attention, through discussion, to the above possibilities and then set them to work again.

CLARIFY *Make a decision about how you are going to convey the feeling of fleeing. You may use one particular way or two or three different ways. Once you have decided, practice, until you can repeat, accurately, your idea.*

GUIDED EXPERIENCE *1. Take a crouched position with your fingers very lightly touching the floor.*
2. Leading very carefully, slowly and cautiously, with one hand, start to move in any direction; forward, sideways, backwards; but keep very low.
Allow time for this to be worked upon.
3. Imagine the floor is covered with very dry leaves, which the slightest movement will stir to noise. Try not to disturb those leaves. Make your actions very slow and precise.

DISCOVER *Now think of the word "stalk". Perform the action we have just done with "stalking" in mind.*
Leave the children with the problem, but be encouraging their awareness of moving very slowly and carefully.

CLARIFY *Take the two words "flee" and "stalk". Put them into an action sentence of your own.*

When the children are working on this problem, observe whether or not the changes between very sudden actions and very slow actions is beginning to dominate. This should be the case, but you may need to find further ways of helping the children to enhance these two contrasting time factors.

GUIDED EXPERIENCE 1. *Find a space and sit down in an asymmetrical position.* (See page 121.)

2. *Using either one or both hands try to capture a moth that has just settled near by. The moth might be on the floor or on an imaginary bush, for example, but it is quite still in one spot.* Watch the children very carefully. Some children make the whole action very slow and delicate as their hands commence to move, approach and surround the moth. Others make the whole action very sudden. Some make a slow approach and, then, at the last second, sudden action to surround the moth. Once the children have worked on the idea, reinforce their awareness by drawing attention to the above three different approaches.

3. *Now decide how you are going to release the moth.*

CLARIFY *Put together your own ideas on capturing and releasing a moth or several moths one after the other.*

Once the children have satisfactorily accomplished this, set them their final problem.

DISCOVER *By yourself, or with a partner, take at least two of the four words we used today: flee, stalk, capture, release; and make them into a sentence of action that satisfies you.*

The lesson is now entirely in the hands of the children, and the situation may well require another lesson for the children to fully develop their ideas.

NOTES TO THE TEACHER

1. This lesson makes use of the earlier learning experiences the children had with action words.

2. Note, particularly, how quickly the children have been set the problem of discovery. This is because the groundwork on action words has given them sound knowledge upon which to draw. With their familiarity with action words, they no longer need spend much time on that aspect of learning. Instead, the time is spent on clarifying the *quality* of the action.

SPACE

As it was possible to observe children becoming more interested in the quality of time and energy, rather than in the performance of a particular action: So too it will be possible to notice how they frequently have a strong preference or attitude towards the spatial quality of movement. As with time and energy, there are two very clear spatial attitudes which children may have. They may prefer the direct, linear, non-deviating attitude towards space; Or, they may prefer a more flexible, meandering, indirect attitude. These are the two opposite but related attitudes which are reflected in action.

Lessons emphasizing the use of a spatial attitude can be developed on similar lines to those using time and energy: working with actions, which contrast with each other in their directness and plasticity; exploring words and sounds, which awaken both our imagination and movement response; working with isolated body parts, with whole body actions, as an individual, with a partner and in a group. All are ways of exploring the quality of space.

These two qualities of space can also be recorded, as were time and energy. Again the symbol that action is present ⟋ forms the basis of the symbols. That the action is direct is written ⌐ and that the action is flexible is written ⌡. Again children can explore interpreting these symbols in many different ways:

A ⌡ group,

A ⌐ arm action,

A phrase of action which is ⌡ ⌡ ⌐⌐

The motion factor of space can be combined with any one of the other motion factors. Consequently it is possible to have actions which are flexible and firm or flexible and finetouch. Alternately, they could be direct and firm, or direct and finetouch. These are combinations of the motion factors of space and energy. Space factors can also be combined with time. The actions then become flexible and sustained; direct and sustained or direct and sudden, flexible and sudden. Once children start combining two motion factors, it is a simple step to combining three factors. Once this occurs they will be exploring complete effort actions.

TIME/ENERGY/SPACE = COMPLETE EFFORT

When all three qualities of action: time, energy and space have been explored by the children they can see quite naturally which of their actions can be clearly defined in all three qualities. An action may be firm, direct, and sudden—three motion factors are present. When

61

all three qualities are present in an action, it is known as a complete effort action. There are eight of these complete effort actions and they again open up a new area of learning exploration and creativity for the children. In addition, children find them exciting and fully comprehensible.

In these eight definitions the word underlined is the name given by Rudolph Laban to each of the eight effort actions. The other words are those which may help to capture the quality of the effort action.

A strong, sudden, direct action	= PUNCH WRENCH CHOP THRUST JERK TUG
A strong, sudden, flexible action	= SLASH WHIP
A strong, sustained, direct action	= PRESS PUSH PULL HEAVE
A strong, sustained, flexible action	= WRING WRITHE
A light, sudden, direct action	= DAB TAP PAT
A light, sustained, direct action	= GLIDE
A light, sudden, flexible action	= FLICK FLUTTER
A light, sustained, flexible action	= FLOAT DRIFT MEANDER

One way to explore these actions with children is to work with pairs of opposites. As white helps to distinguish black, so directly opposing effort actions make each other clearer by comparison. Also, physically, it is easier to master opposites rather than actions which are closely allied to each other. For example; flick is the complete opposite of press, whereas float is closely associated with flick, changing only in time factor. From Grades 4 to 6 there should be a natural development in the ability to distinguish and use the different qualities of movement.

Grade IV

The distinction between the separate factors involved in time, energy and space, should be fostered. The ability to use sudden and sustained actions, firm and finetouch actions, flexible and direct actions can be expected; although transitions between these may be difficult. A vocabulary of words descriptive of these qualities should be built. Excited, staccato, powerful, smooth, lingering, and urgent are a few effective words. Associating qualities with specific sounds from percussion, voice and music is possible. Combinations of two qualities are common, and sudden/strong or flexible/firm, for example, can be very clearly executed. The teacher should expose the children to many of the combinations of *two qualities* and should put these into suitable pairs of opposites, for example, a sudden/flexible action contrasted with a sustained/direct action.

Qualities can be distinguished in whole body actions, positions of stillness and in body parts.

Group work and partner work can be developed showing one quality or two contrasting qualities.

Grade V

These children should be able to master all of the work for Grade 4 and, in addition, they should be able to combine the qualities of time, energy and space into the complete effort actions. They should also be able to perform the eight effort actions and to use them in whole body actions or in isolated body parts. They can work with pairs of opposite actions, for example, float and punch.

Plenty of opportunity should be given to develop these effort actions with partners and in groups. Improvisations and dances based on effort actions should play an important part in the lessons.

Grade VI

The work for Grades 4 and 5 should have been mastered and, in addition, the children should be able to show that they can work with two effort actions which show a change of only one quality. For example, they can change the space quality between float and glide without changing the other two qualities (time and energy). In this way they start to recognize space-rhythm.

They start to recognize and produce changes of time-rhythm by changing the time quality. For example, flick, flick, flick, float; changing the time quality brings out a recognizable rhythm.

They can also produce changes of energy-rhythm by changing

from qualities of press to glide. This has however been found to be a most difficult change for the children to experience.

This interplay between different rhythms resulting from the transition between one effort action and another should be explored fully by individual children. Experiences can then be structured for group work, including interaction between groups. At this stage it is simpler for the children within a group to work with the same group activity.

Finally, in reconsidering why children should be educated in the use of these "effort" actions, it is essential to remember that movement is a fundamental form of communication. Communication is man's greatest capacity and greatest need. The greater man's and children's understanding and control of movement as a communicative force in life, the greater his freedom. Exploring and mastering the full range of quality in actions, as it is found in a study of the eight basic effort actions, provides children with more experience of the communicative powers of movement. The presentation of the material must, however, be at the children's level of interest, understanding and needs.

This chapter attempts to give teachers both the necessary knowledge and understanding of the qualities of movement to use them in an expressive way and to show them some of the ways of presenting this material. Once the teacher and class become alive to this aspect of movement they will find, constantly, that there are ideas they want to explore, music to interpret, verse and story to which they want to dance.

REFERENCES

Preston, Valerie Dunlop. *A Handbook for Modern Educational Dance*. London: Macdonald and Evans Ltd., 1963.

Preston, Dunlop, and Valerie. *Practical Kinetography Laban*. London: Macdonald and Evans Ltd., 1969.

Russell, Joan. *Creative Dance in the Secondary School*. London: Macdonald and Evans Ltd., 1969.

Laban, Rudolf. *Modern Educational Dance*. Second edition. London: Macdonald and Evans Ltd., 1963.

MUSIC REFERENCES

Lesson 6: "Slashing and Punching" by Ada Heynssen. From *Modern Dance Record Number 1*. London: Macdonald and Evans Ltd.

Lesson 7: "Gliding and Floating" by Ada Heynssen. From *Modern Dance Record Number 1*. London: Macdonald and Evans Ltd.

3

SPACE

Appreciation of the use of space in dance comes from the growing awareness of, and ability to feel, movement as a three-dimensional form. The body expresses itself three dimensionally both when it is in a static, held position and when it creates patterns in the air as it moves through space. In one aspect, only, can the dancer's use of space be likened to that of painting or flat-art forms—in the floor patterns created, which are, of necessity, two dimensional. To be fully alive to the possibilities of designing actions in space, places considerable intellectual and emotional demand upon the child. The child between eight and twelve years of age can, however, handle concepts of space if presented in a concrete and realistic way. From there he can progress to a more sophisticated understanding of the use of space in movement.

The concepts of space which can be developed during the fourth, fifth and sixth grades build upon the elementary space concepts of extension, direction, level, and pathway which the children have studied in the earlier grades. Again, if these concepts in dance have not been studied previously, it will be necessary for the children to be given an understanding of their application to dance. For this purpose these aspects are included in the movement analysis of space found in Chapter 5. The intellectual level of the children in Grades 4 to 6 normally permits them to apply, very quickly, the concepts of size, direction, level and pathway, which have been acquired in other areas of study, to the dance work. The concepts of air pattern, floor pattern, focus, and the beginning of spatial directions, are more advanced concepts which can now be studied in Grades 4 to 6. The following concepts give to the dance its spatial design. These can only be developed by increasing the awareness of the children to how they are moving in space and how it feels to be concentrating on space.

AN AWARENESS OF FLOOR PATTERN
AND DESIGN

The floor pattern of a dance is made by the invisible tracks left by the child as he moves. These tracks or floor patterns are being constantly made in life but we are seldom aware of them. In dance, the objective is to become aware of the pattern being made on the floor and to select a pattern which will enhance the total design and expression of the dance. It is extremely important that the teacher help the children to become aware of how a floor pattern "feels". To set them superficial problems of cutting designs on the floor is not enough. For example, a problem might be set to reproduce the following pattern on the floor:

This problem could be used in several ways. The children, in moving to produce the floor pattern could consider that the pattern could be started at either end of the spiral; they could become aware of the different sensations of tightening and closure as they moved towards the center of the spiral, and opening and freedom as they move toward the outside of the spiral.

For the child answering this problem it is essential that he be guided to become aware of, and experience, the above responses.

It is evident that floor pattern is not only design, but does, in fact, by its selection, produce certain movement sensations and consequently expression. Only when considered for both of these values can floor pattern have a significant learning experience embodied within it.

AN AWARENESS OF AIR PATTERN
AND DESIGN

Whereas the floor pattern is two dimensional, the air pattern has the greater freedom of using three dimensions. To distinguish between the sculptural design which the mass of the body creates as it occupies space, an air pattern must be considered as a moving pattern. Whereas a held twisted body shape will have a design in space, it is only when motion takes place, that an air pattern will be created. For example, the pattern of the spiral now taken as an air pattern could have several answers:

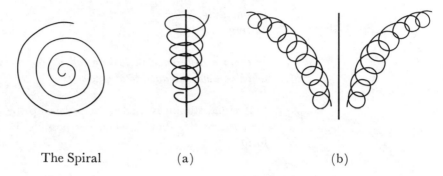

The Spiral   (a)   (b)

The body could be used as a central spoke which pivoted to allow the arms to cut the spiral pattern in space. (a)

The body could remain on one spot while the arms cut the spiral in front or to the side of the body. (b)

A floor pattern could be created with the spiral air pattern placed on top of the floor pattern. (c)

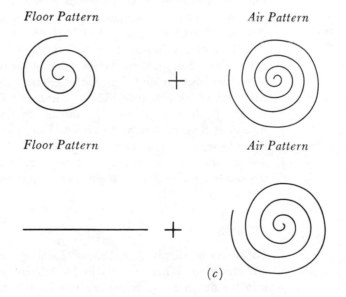

Floor Pattern   *Air Pattern*

Floor Pattern   *Air Pattern*

(*c*)

These are three possible answers. Again an awareness of the feel, the sensation, and the expression created by the air pattern should be heightened. This can be done by such simple questions as:
Could you close your eyes and feel the design you have just made? Which of these words would best describe the feel of your spiral?
closed
open
surrounding
cutting

Is there a difference in feeling when you are inside the spiral and when you cut one outside of yourself?

If visual stimuli is used to help develop the children's concept of air patterns this should, whenever possible, be in three dimensional form.

FLOOR PATTERN AND AIR PATTERN

These two factors will always be present in movement, except when the body is anchored to one spot and movement occurs above that spot. The children should be given time to adequately experience, absorb and learn about one aspect before going on to the other. Later it is possible to be aware of combinations of floor and air patterns in all their complexity. It is, however, recommended that this area of work come in Junior High or even Senior High School.

It is important that the teacher does not confuse direction with air pattern and floor pattern. When working on pattern it is better to avoid reference to direction. Consider one simple example of the confusion which can arise: The children in a dance lesson are continually circling the room. The teacher thinks of this as direction instead of floor pattern and frequently suggests to the children that they change direction. They change direction but continue to circle and the teacher has not helped them to resolve the problem. What she wants them to alter is their floor pattern, not their direcion.

FOCUS

Focus can be simply described as "looking" and concerns distance and direction. When a child in his movement looks forward and into the distance and maintains this focus for a time, he is giving his action a spatial focus. The observer is drawn to the expression of attention on the distant spot and expects this to have some immediate connection with the movement or dance.

Consider someone about to buy something he considers of great value. He will frequently focus on the object and, while maintaining this focus, go through many changes of action and posture. The observer is in no doubt as to the object being considered and is often given a non-verbal commentary on the emotional and intellectual processes through which the person is going. The object is outside of the person and is spatially connected to him by focus. "Hide and seek" is very much a focus game for the seeker, and such simple analogy can readily explain to children the importance of "looking" when they compose actions, sequences and compositions in dance.

SPATIAL ACTIONS

Spatial actions occur in dance when direction is emphasized. Moving upward brings about rising; downward—a sinking action; to the right and left—an opening or closing action; forward or backward —advancing and retreating actions.

These are basic spatial actions rather than body actions. The concentration and attention of the child has to be upon space in order to convey the significance of the action. A child can be standing with arms extended upward and head thrown back yet not convey the attitude and feeling of rising. This is because he has cut himself off from the space above him and he is not reaching upward into it. In all of spatial action, the teacher has to help the children to feel not only the action but the space with which the action is concerned. Action words in Chapter 1 can be used, but this other dimension must be added as children explore rising, spreading, shrinking, opening, reaching, contracting. These actions should be felt from the center and employ the entire body. (If body parts, only, are used to isolate the action, those parts should have the capacity for being used in a way similar to the whole body. Hands which open, close, spread, rise, sink, are more conducive to producing the sensation of the spatial action than legs.) Group work helps the children to feel that they can surround and close away from open space, open and expand in space, fall, sink, advance and withdraw.

These four areas: floor patterns, air patterns, focus, and spatial actions are, consequently, the major areas to be considered in Grades 4 to 6. They build upon the simpler concepts of size, direction, level, pathway and space words, studied in Grades 1 to 3, and precede the work on dimensional and diagonal scales; door, wheel and table planes, central and peripheral transitions, which will be studied in Junior and Senior High School.

An excellent method of introducing children to design is through the use of visual aids. For the following lessons a selection of transparencies, colour cards and mobiles were made. These were used as the initial stimuli and the children were given freedom in selection of the designs with which they worked. The visual aids were used in the following order:

Lesson 1: A transparency upon which three distinct colours were used as background to three simple designs: These could easily be made in the form of colour charts.

Red   Yellow   Blue

Lesson 2: Three colour cards were used which could be fitted together in different order. To achieve this, the design on each card must end in the same place: These designs represent but single examples, more can be found in lesson 2.

Card I   Card II   Card III

Lesson 3: Two colour cards were used. One depicting several circles and one a radiating design.

These cards are so designed as to be used individually or in any order. The problem set can consequently be varied in complexity.

Although in these lessons the designs are presented on transparencies or colour cards, three dimensional models would be equally if not more effective.

The lessons as presented are an illustration of how the subject might be approached in each grade. Lesson 1 is for Grade 4; lesson 2 is for Grade 5 and lesson 3 is for Grade 6. They could also be taken as a developmental sequence of three lessons provided appropriate modification of vocabulary and experiences was made.

Lesson 1

Material of the lesson / To develop the children's awareness of how actions can make designs in space both on the floor and in the air.

GUIDED EXPERIENCE

1. *Choose any action from running, jumping, skipping, hopping, and make "tracks" all over the floor.*
2. *This time, start from one spot. Make a very clear track or design on the floor which goes away from the spot and then comes back to it.*
3. *Remember your own track or design on the floor and come and look at another three.*

The three designs shown above are then presented either on the overhead projector, or on the chalk board or on colour cards:

DISCOVER

Choose one of these designs. Go and cut it so clearly on the floor that we can all see which one you have chosen.

Allow time for the children to explore this idea and give them help with the following suggestions:

a) *change the size of the pattern,*
b) *know where it starts and finishes,*
c) *use different actions to create the pattern,*
d) *change or vary the speed of making the pattern.*

These activities are not designed merely to add variety to the initial problem but to reinforce the understanding of floor pattern. Each of the variations will add a different problem to the initial one. It is the teacher's responsibility to keep the attention focused on the floor pattern.

CLARIFY   *Choose from your ideas which floor pattern you would like to show. Practice it a few times until you are completely satisfied with it.*

GUIDED EXPERIENCE   *1. These patterns can also be made in the air. You can make a very small pattern in the air with one finger. See if you can make several very small patterns all around you.*
2. You can stand inside a pattern and make it all around yourself. Try it.
3. You can leap into the air, or run and leap and make these patterns in mid-air. Try and make this design in the air:

CLARIFY   *Imagine what the movement of an enormous red paint brush would be if it painted your design. Some parts would be large and bold, some parts small and delicate, some parts would be on the floor, some in the air, but the design would be very clear. Decide where you are going to start. Paint your design, and then put a full stop at the end.*
Allow the children time to work out this final product.

NOTES TO THE TEACHER

1. The first two guided experiences are intended to involve the children in activity and at the same time start to bring their attention to floor designs. As soon as this has been done, the designs should be presented on the overhead projector.
2. The first guided experience gives greater freedom of movement than the second, but will not produce clarity of floor patterns. Consequently, the second guided experience is more structured.
3. Once the designs have been shown to the children, in Grade 4, they very soon exhaust the possibilities within them. Showing your designs to partners and other suggestions included in the lesson can help the children to overcome the movement problems and clarify their ideas, quickly.
4. Placing the responsibility for decisions of both selections and standard on the individual children is extremely important. They will need constant encouragement to raise their own standards of expectations, but the teacher should always be working towards intrinsic motivation on the part of the children.
5. At times, a limited amount of imagery, used wisely, can help the children produce the design and the quality the teacher is seeking. The important factor is to express this imagery to the children so that it does not detract from the quality of their potential movements, nor be too limiting.

72

Grade V

Lesson 2

Material of the lesson / To develop a sequence of different designs in the air and on the floor.

GUIDED EXPERIENCE

1. *Take several leaping actions but as you leap, try to make a triangle with the floor as the base.*

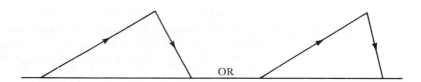

2. *As you leap try to be aware of the angular pathway you are making in the air, rather than concerning yourself with the action of your jump.*

Give the children time to work on this energetic activity and note some of the successful attempts.

DISCOVER

Keep the idea of a triangular or angular shape being cut through space and see what other actions will cut this shape out of space. You might try more with the upper part of the body or instead try to get the action in the legs.

CLARIFY

Now, instead of the children clarifying their actions, the teacher should stress the importance of being aware of how designs are made in space. See Note to Teacher (following) for explanation.

GUIDED EXPERIENCE

Create, with movement, a floor pattern which consists of a series of connected boxes.

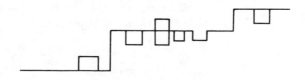

The actions may be of your own choice but the floor pattern must be boxes.

73

DISCOVER   *Take a partner and try to discover whether or not he really makes a series of connecting boxes.*

CLARIFY   *You have now made two patterns: an air pattern, which was angular; and a floor pattern, which consisted of boxes. Put these into a sequence, in any order, and try to find out if there is any difference in the movement sensations of each.*

Give the children time to work on this and then find out if the children felt that there was any noticeable difference in the movement sensation of each pattern. It is quite probable that they will say that the box pattern was mechanical, restricted, machine-like and that the triangle was powerful, arrow-like and penetrating. This should be used to further explain how patterns on the floor and in the air do produce certain movement sensations.

GUIDED EXPERIENCE   *Try one more pattern which you may select to do either as a floor pattern or an air pattern.*

Once the children have had time to work on this pattern they should be set their final problem.

CLARIFY   *Clarify a sentence of the three patterns. They may be placed in any order.*

Once the children have clarified this sentence they should be encouraged to explain how the third pattern was different in movement sensation from the other two. It is more rounded, smooth, peaceful and flowing.

NOTES TO THE TEACHER

When explaining to the children why they are turning their attention to space, the following points should be made:
1. All movement has a design or a pattern in the same way that all buildings have a form or structure.

2. Actions such as run, twirl, roll are the materials of the building of the dance, but these must be designed into a definite shape.

3. An important part of the spatial design of an action or a dance is being aware of how it looks in space.

4. Being aware of how a design looks in space can help us express our idea, mood, composition, story more clearly.

Grade VI

Lesson 3

Material of the lesson / Space designs with a partner.

GUIDED EXPERIENCE

1. *Choose partners. One of you act as the leader while the other follows. Cut a series of complete circles, or closed curves, on the floor. As you cut them, give some thought to:*

a) *the varying sizes of the circles,*
b) *the fact that the circles may overlap,*
c) *the clarity of your floor design.*

2. Once you have established a simple floor design, change over the leadership. The new leader should make different circles and designs in the air.

Once the children have had time to develop both ideas, follow up with discussion and questions.

Where would you make the most circles, in the air or on the floor? What are the main characteristics of a circle?

3. Join right hands with your partner and pull away gently from each other, reaching out with your left hand. Make sure that neither one of you pulls so hard that you over-balance your partner. Slowly start to rotate, feeling the circle that you are cutting with your outside hands.

DISCOVER

Stay joined together. Find another way you can cut a circular design in space or on the floor.

DISCUSSION

So far you have been working on a simple circle design. You have made it on the floor, in the air and enlarged it by being joined together. Sometimes it cut through the air; sometimes the circle enclosed a space.

GUIDED EXPERIENCE

Join with another pair, and, in your fours, see what designs you can make on the floor and in the air that radiate outwards from a central point. Your air, or floor, patterns will have a similar design to this:

The children by this time have experienced the concept of space design and how it can be produced by one person, or two people acting together. By being free to evolve their own ideas, they will bring to their work many exciting and imaginative situations.

The teacher now should observe the children's work as they evolve their ideas and help them to bring about a satisfactory movement conclusion.

When a situation is put to the children in this way, they may have problems in getting started. The teacher should not allow the children to flounder for too long or they will lose all interest in the problem. The following material will help to guide the children if this situation occurs.

GUIDED EXPERIENCE
1. *Make a very close and small group near the floor. Gradually cut the space and grow outward to this rhythm: ta, ta, ta, taaaa. . . .*
2. *Pull back in again in your own time.*
This experience should be repeated several times and then the following changes made:
3. *Instead of all four of you spoking out at once, go one at a time:*
No. 1. *ta, ta, ta, taaaaa.*
No. 2. *ta, ta, ta, taaaaa.*
No. 3. *ta, ta, ta, taaaaa.*
No. 4. *ta, ta, ta, taaaaa.*
All come back together.

DISCOVER
Those were two possibilities for answering the design problem. Now see if you can find two more. Remember you may concentrate on the floor design or the air design. Make your selection from your own ideas or from the one practiced as a class. Crystallize the action so that it really is a radiating design in both looks and expansion.

NOTES TO THE TEACHER

In the discussion about circles many of the points mentioned for Lesson 1 (see page 71) could be brought out. In addition, the following should be emphasized: the completeness of a circle; that it must end where it started; that the circle encloses an area of space as well as cutting a circular pathway. When the children are discovering how to cut circles joined together, the following may occur or be encouraged:
1. Two hands joined when facing; here the back should feel the cutting of the circle in space, and the feet the cutting of the circle on the floor.
2. A right hand and left hand link, producing an extension of the follow-the-leader situation.
3. One child may act as a pivot around which the other child revolves.
4. To produce the rhythm for the children to grow outward in space, use a tambour. Beat the rhythm with three simple interspaced beats, and then a longer and louder roll.
5. Whenever the teacher has given the children a problem to work on, he must be able to give structured guidance in solving the problem should this become necessary. Any problem in which the teacher could not give this should not be presented to the children.

FOCUS

The following three lessons on *focus* have been formulated to lead into a dance-drama situation. In dance-drama, the events of the dance unfold in the form of a story. The lessons are developed one for each grade but again they may be adapted for a grade other than that suggested.

Grade IV

Lesson 4

Material of the lesson / To increase the children's awareness of focus using a game of imaginary "Hide and Seek".

GUIDED EXPERIENCE

With a partner, show me what you would do if you were playing Hide and Seek. You may not use any obstacles in the room to hide behind, under or in.

Once the children have shown you, spontaneously, their reactions to this, discuss with them "looking".

DISCUSSION

In that game I saw two kinds of looking. One when the hider appeared to look out from behind something, and one when the seeker was looking for his partner. The difference in these was in the timing. The hider gave very quick, short looks and then drew back into hiding. The searcher gave longer, slower looks and then went forward, paused and looked in another direction.

GUIDED EXPERIENCE

1. *Change over, the hider becoming the seeker. Have another try at reproducing the idea of hide and seek, but make it very clear where and when you are looking.*
Allow time for the children to work on this.
2. *Stop your game for a moment. Show me some of the positions you were in when you were looking.*
3. *On each beat of the drum, show me a position you had, and exactly how you were looking. Were you looking up, forward, a long way away, quite close to you?*

CLARIFY

1. *Hider: Clarify your starting position, how you travelled and then hid. Did you run, skip, jump, tiptoe to your hiding place? Did you go straight there, or did you make a curving or zig-zag path on the way? Show very clearly the looking at the beginning—focusing on your hiding place as you travel towards it—and where you are looking when you hide.*
2. *Seeker: Clarify how you started. How you travelled when looking for your partner, and how many times you paused to look.*

78

GUIDED EXPERIENCE   *The story needs to have an ending. Try these: the seeker finds the hider; the seeker does not find the hider. Freeze at the end of your story and show very clearly what happened.*

CLARIFY   *Work through your complete story:*
a) The hider leaves and travels and hides,
b) The seeker comes looking and pausing and looking,
c) An interplay of hiding and seeking,
d) Your own ending.

NOTES TO THE TEACHER

The children can become very absorbed in dancing out this story and they may lose their concentration on focus. The teacher can help them to maintain it by being clear and continually attending to and drawing out the "looking" part of the story.

Grade V

Lesson 5

Material of the lesson / To develop a dance on focus, using a group of three.

GUIDED EXPERIENCE   *1. In a group of three, form a line, either one behind the other, or side by side.*
2. All of you look towards the same spot and concentrate.
3. Move towards, away from, and around that spot, retaining your line. Use the following rhythm: jump—jump, jump, jump—jump.
Allow the children time to experiment with the idea.

DISCOVER   *1. Continue moving but try to keep your eye focused on the spot the whole time.*
2. When you are moving away you must still maintain eye contact, even if your back is turned to the spot.

GUIDED EXPERIENCE   *1. This time, in your threes, try running and leaping over the spot. All the time you must look at it.*
2. Take it in turns to leap over the spot. The two who are not leaping, increase the tension by continuing to watch the spot.

DISCOVER   *1. Find out how you can combine the first sequence; jump—jump, jump, jump—jump—with the running and leaping sequence.*
2. You may change the order around, but never lose the focus.

DISCUSSION   *You have tried two ideas which we might use in a ritual dance. A ritual dance is often performed as part of a ceremony: a hunt, wed-*

79

ding, funeral, or festival. Its pattern is always the same, can be re-peated, and is passed down from one generation to another. The ritual is usually very dramatic and exciting. You have already pro-duced two dramatic sequences which could be the beginning of your ritual. Now let us work on a third part.

GUIDED EXPERIENCE

The third part of your ritual must follow the following design:
Travel—focus
Travel—focus
Travel—focus
Travel—close in.
You may bring this about in any way you wish, providing you clearly show these four events.
The children should be given time to work on this, and the following suggestions may be needed to help some groups:
a) *How do you travel, with which action?*
b) *Do you travel as a group, in one direction?*
c) *Do you travel individually?*
d) *What is your group shape when focusing?*
e) *Is your focus stationary or does it, too, travel?*
f) *When you close in are you focusing inward towards a central spot or outward in different directions?*

CLARIFY

Once the children have evolved this part of the dance, the complet-ed ritual should be danced. This could be accompanied either by drumming or by an appropriate musical selection. The ritual will contain a sequence decided by the children. For example:
Jump—jump, jump, jump—jump
Run—leap—run—leap
Travel—focus—travel—focus
Travel—focus—travel—close in.

Grade VI

Lesson 6

Material of the lesson / To create a dance comedy in which focus is used as the main movement idea. The dance could be called, "Do you see what I see?"

GUIDED EXPERIENCE

You have all, at some time or another, been walking down the street and stopped to look at something interesting. Sometimes you stop for a long time and sometimes you hardly pause at all.
2. Take a simple running action and, when you hear the drum beat, focus on some imaginary point of interest.

80

Repeat several times.

3. Without the drum beat, and using different actions from running, choose how and when you pause and focus.

4. Instead of moving from one place to another, stay in one spot. Focus on one thing and try to draw attention to it. Here are two ways in which you can show this:

a) change your own position, to kneeling, sitting or lying, while looking at the same spot.

b) repeat an action; stamp on the floor, pointing again and again.

CLARIFY *Make a sentence of travelling. Focus—travel—focus—draw attention to the focus.*

GUIDED EXPERIENCE *In a group of five see if you can work out the following situation:*

1. Two of you establish something of interest to look at. You show clearly, by your focus and body position, that you are both looking at the same thing.

2. You are joined by Numbers 3 and 4, who also start looking at the same thing. Then Number 1 leaves.

3. Along comes Number 5, who joins 2, 3, and 4, and starts looking. Numbers 2, 3, and 4 leave Number 5, looking by himself.

Once the children have experimented with, and grasped the idea of, the fluctuating group numbers, help them to clarify their ideas into a dance sequence.

CLARIFY *1. How do you approach your focus?*

2. What do you do to make it really a point of interest?

3. How long do you stay before leaving?

4. What is your group shape like when focusing? How does it change?

5. How do you finally leave the group? In what position is Number 5 left?

The teacher should try to help the children to find a sense of rhythm in their actions, rather than allowing the sequence to develop into a purely dramatic situation.

NOTES TO THE TEACHER

1. The focusing situation can be varied, but, however you decide to establish it, the problem should be clearly understood. The essence of the situation is to let two children start everything and get the other three involved. Eventually one is left alone, not sure what he is looking at.

2. In the three lessons on focus, the situations could also lead to developing clarity in floor design. In "Hide and Seek" what is the

floor pattern? Similarly, in "Ritual" and "Do you see what I see" what floor patterns are being made? Again it is necessary to emphasize that the teacher must be quite clear as to her objectives in any lesson. The learning situation must be objectively presented or the systematic study of movement with its closely interwoven strands will be lost in a lack of content structure.

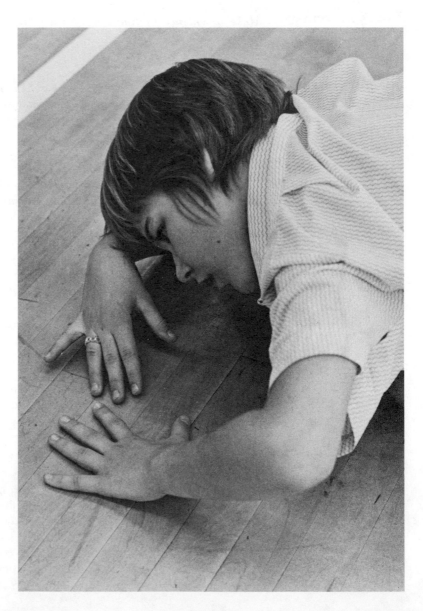

BASIC SPATIAL ACTIONS

The following three lessons on the basic spatial actions show the development of one action/pair in each of the grades. Rising and sinking is developed with Grade 4, advancing and retreating with Grade 5, and opening and closing with Grade 6. This selection is made because certain of the basic spatial actions are especially suited as beginning actions for the younger children. It must be stressed that the work with these actions is an introduction, only, and they would not be dealt with in depth until Junior or Senior High School.

A different approach is used in the following three lessons. Each lesson is divided into two separate parts: The first is outlined and the second is left for the teacher to develop. The intention is to help student or beginning teachers to become confident in their own ability to continue with ideas for creative dance.

Grade IV

Lesson 7

Material of the lesson / To explore the basic spatial actions of rising and sinking emphasizing different body parts.
Accompaniment: Band 4, Side 2, *Electronic Sound Patterns* by Daphne Oram.

PART I
GUIDED EXPERIENCE

1. *Find a position near to the floor. Look outward towards the ceiling or the walls.*
2. *Feel that position is connecting you by an invisible thread with the points where you are looking.*
3. *Very slowly, to the sound of the drum, be drawn towards that spot in a rising action.*
4. *Hold your position for a second and then quickly withdraw back to the floor.*

DISCOVER

Work on the idea of being drawn upward and outward towards the ceiling or walls by this magnetic force in space. The force holds you there for a second, then lets you go.
Ensure that the children are feeling the connection with space. This can be seen by observing the concentration outward and the feeling of reaching into space.

GUIDED EXPERIENCE

1. *Keep the feeling of rising towards a magnetic force in space but use only a body part—a head, hand, foot, back.*
Allow the children time to work with the idea of body parts rising.
2. *Listen to this very short piece of music. You can hear the sound being drawn out into space and then quickly recoiling.*

83

DISCOVER

Keep the phrase of music in your head. Put together a sentence of rising—recoiling—rising—recoiling—rising.

FORMULATE

Put together your sentence of action with the music. Be able to repeat what you have created.

PART II
GUIDED EXPERIENCE

The first part of the lesson has emphasized the rising. Using another band from the same record, develop the feeling of sinking. Band 1, Side 1, is suggested for this. Following this exploration, the children should be guided in using both the rising and sinking actions as active parts in a simple dance. For this, Band 3, Side 2, is recommended.

Grade V

Lesson 8

Material of the lesson / To develop the actions of advancing and retreating in a partner and group situation.
Accompaniment: Band 4 or 5, Side 1, *Electronic Sound Patterns* by Daphne Oram.

PART I
GUIDED EXPERIENCE

1. Everyone gather into the center of the room and concentrate upon the center spot.
2. Produce a feeling of tension by leaning towards the center; keep concentrating and looking towards the spot all the time.
3. Emphasizing any body part—hip, head, foot, back; suddenly make that part pull backwards away from the center.
4. Let one part pull back, then another, until you have to step backwards and retreat. Keep this retreating going as you pull away farther and farther from the center.
5. Come to the center again and once more try retreating, but at the same time listen to the music that accompanies this retreating.
(Band 4)

DISCOVER

As a group, start very still and tense, focusing on the center. Feel how you can retreat as a group, and create an atmosphere with your group action.

GUIDED EXPERIENCE

1. This time, from a standing position anywhere in the room, develop the following travelling sequence: step forward—step forward—leap backward. The stepping action is an emphasized walking

84

action and the leap backward lands on two feet.

2. Develop this pattern anywhere in the room, but emphasize the stepping forward and leaping backwards. Keep the rhythm going evenly, but make a slight pause after the leap.

3. Listen to the sounds on the record and let your stepping and leaping accompany the sounds. (Band 5)

Allow the children time to develop this rhythm with the music. Encourage a feeling of strength and tension in their whole bodies.

DISCOVER

1. With a partner, use a meeting and parting situation to develop the step—step—leap pattern.

2. As you develop your idea bring about the impression that you are advancing toward and retreating from your partner.

In this part of the lesson the children can be led to discover the different situations which can occur from:

a) starting apart or together,

b) starting facing or back to back,

c) advancing with steps and retreating with leaps,

d) advancing with leaps and retreating with steps.

PART II
GUIDED EXPERIENCE

These two aspects of the lesson have been developed separately. The teacher should now attempt to join these two experiences into one dance. The bands can either be used in the order in which they occur on the record, or can be taped in reversed order.

NOTES TO THE TEACHER

Encourage the feeling of advancing and retreating in the children's movement by stressing the stepping forward with the legs leading, and the retreating with the center of the body in the leap.

It is difficult for *all* children to concentrate in creating group movement. They can however, be greatly helped by the teacher's own involvement and concentration.

Grade VI

Lesson 9

Material of the lesson / To develop the actions of opening and closing using the following verse:

ACHOO!
Squeeze the sneeze!
There's fungus
Amongus.[2]

[2]Bob Dyck, Grade 9, from *Fluid Filosophies of Future Fools.* (Edmonton, Alberta: A. O'Dwyer and G. Whitney, 1969).

85

PART I

GUIDED EXPERIENCE

1. *Find a space in the room and take a kneeling, sitting, or standing position.*
2. *From that position, squeeze your ribs, arms, back, inward and deflate your lungs.*
3. *Suddenly release the squeeze and let your lungs expand, your arms and ribs fling open.*
4. *Repeat the squeezing and releasing several times.*

DISCOVER

As you are doing this, how can you make the releasing action really spread open and travel into space?

If at this point the teacher indicates with a gripping and releasing of the hands, the feeling of flinging into space, the children will be better able to capture the essence of the opening action.

FORMULATE

Create a rhythmical sentence of squeezing and releasing. The first part of the sentence should be small. Gradually increase in size until the squeezing and releasing are very large.

GUIDED EXPERIENCE

Find a group of five. Try to solve this movement problem: using only squeezing and releasing actions, individually and as a group, accompany or interpret the sound, "ACHOO!".

Give the children time to work on this problem, making it clear that they can either make the sound as they move, or convey the idea of the word through movements alone.

OBSERVATION

Find another group and watch each other. Notice whether you see mainly squeezing and releasing actions.

GUIDED EXPERIENCE

1. *Find a space for your group somewhere in the room and stand, sit, or kneel apart from each other.*
2. *Be aware of the space that the group is using. Look around, know where you are placed in the group and how it looks.*
3. *As a group, move and decrease your space. Squeeze the space out from between you until you become a very close-knit group.*

DISCOVER

Try that idea sereval times until you feel that the group is really squeezing out the space. Find out how your body has to close, as you and the group close or squeeze together.

GUIDED EXPERIENCE

1. *You have worked on the word "ACHOO!" and found a group squeezing out the space. Find out how your body has to close, as you ing or closing space. Add also the words, "Squeeze the sneeze!"*
2. *Your sentence of action now accompanies:*

ACHOO!
Squeeze the sneeze!

Allow time for the group to make the connections with the movement sequences. Each group will do this in its own way.

PART II
GUIDED EXPERIENCE   For the second part of this lesson the teacher should design experiences to accompany:

There's fungus
Amongus.

Two suggestions for this are to help the children:
a) explore interpreting the words very slowly and almost mysteriously, as the group spreads into space.
b) explore interpreting the words very quickly and with much agitation, as the group quickly closes together.
    Finally, the groups should be able to perform a very short dance sequence to all of the lines.

REFERENCES

Russell, Joan. *Modern Dance in Education.* London: Macdonald and Evans Ltd., 1958.
Hawkins, Alma. *Creating through Dance.* New Jersey: Prentice-Hall, Inc., 1964.

MUSIC REFERENCES

Lessons 7 and 8: Daphne Oram, *Electronic Sound Patterns:* "Listen, Move and Dance", Number 3. E.M.I. Records Limited No. 7EG8762.

4

RELATIONSHIPS

The earlier chapters have used situations demanding two, three, four or more participants. Although these learning situations have not centered around relationships, the children have, in fact, been involved in becoming aware of working with others.

What does the term, relationships, mean in creative dance, and does it differ from the term as it is used in everyday life?

Children are involved in changing relationships every day of their school lives. Friendships are made which endure, other friendships are made which are quickly broken. The social climate of any class will inevitably influence what can be achieved in the dance lesson. A feud can make it impossible to develop a dance which demands co-operation between the feuding participants. Equally, dance may ease a conflicting relationship. The teacher, however, has to recognize the social development and changing relationship of the children and present dance material which can be accepted by them without jeopardizing, or challenging too strongly, their existing beliefs and friendships.

The wise teacher is not going to insist upon the children carrying out a dance based on a relationship which is completely contrary to the existing climate in the class. Her lesson must be sufficiently flexible to allow the children to manoeuvre within the problem, and so find partnerships, groups and situations within which they can acceptably work. Relationship situations in dance can often complement and recreate the ever-changing pattern of relationships found in a normal classroom. The situations of meeting, parting, regrouping, harmonizing, and conflicting found in day-to-day school life are also found in the relationships of creative dance.

Yet the relationships in dance are not these situations or emotions in their truest sense. In dance, the children extract and control these relationship situations. An "angry group" will have extracted and controlled the actions and moods of anger, and will be selecting appropriate movements to convey their expression. Dance relationship can be highly significant as a medium for helping children to understand and control everyday feeling and events, but they must be skillfully structured. To set a relationship problem which asks to "show me a happy group" is doomed to failure. A problem which helps the children to extract the actions, pathways, time and energy factors of a "happy group" then, through understanding these qualities, to bring about the desired expression, can be both educative and successful.

The essential difference between the everyday relationship and the dance relationship is that the latter is the outcome of observation and scientific enquiry. The former is less controlled, and more simply an outcome of casual happenings. Relationships, however, are not so much a body of knowledge to be learned, as an essential part of increasing our awareness and sensitivity towards others.

The following lesson plans are an attempt to suggest how practical tasks, questioning and discussion might help the children become more aware of their partnerships or groups and learn to respond in each situation with an increased awareness. They also are a guide for the teacher in this sensitive area, and she must present situations which will help the child to become aware of how he is affecting his partner or a group while giving him some control over these factors.

Relationships can be experienced within one year in many different groupings: partner-work, and work in both small and large groups. The development of group-work is not a hierarchy, it is not necessary to be able to work with a partner before working in a large group. The tendency to develop relationships hierarchically— partner-work, trio-work, or group-work, stems only from the readiness or entering behaviour of the child. Consequently, a child in Grade 1 may only be able to work in simple partner situations because of his stage of readiness. The entering behaviour of the children in the upper elementary is such that partner work, trios, small and large groups can all be experienced in all of these areas. The situation set, though, may have to vary in degree of complexity. The material on relationships, which follows, presents one lesson plan in each of the relationship areas. This plan is given in order to guide the teacher in a possible way of developing a lesson on relationships. The lesson is then followed by suggestions for further developing that particular area of the work.

The following areas of relationship can be studied in both partner or group work in Grades 4 to 6:

1. Meeting and parting,
2. Meeting and staying together,
3. Leading and following,
4. Shadowing and mirroring,
5. Action and response,
6. Relating to shape, relating to quality, relating to touch.

91

Again these situations should not be considered as a hierarchal development. They can be presented in any order to a class but the situations will have to be appropriate for the readiness level of that particular group of children.

MEETING AND PARTING, MEETING AND STAYING TOGETHER

These events happen every day as people meet, greet each other, perhaps stay together for a while, and then part. Each meeting, parting, and staying will have its own meaning for the people involved. They may feel pleasure, surprise, annoyance, wish to linger in each other's presence, or to be on their way. Each situation and mood will have its own quality which will be seen in the body action, the facial expression, and the spatial relationship of the people who meet.

Looking at a painting, we capture much of its meaning and mood from the figures caught in stillness. We gain a suggestion of what has gone before and anticipate what may happen in the future to the figures caught upon the canvas. Three figures sitting side by side on a log facing the ocean indicate a relationship by the turn of a head, the inclination of a body. Watching, we are less absorbed by the action than by the interplay between the three. Poets and novelists constantly evoke the meeting, parting and staying together of people in order to give suspense, interest and colour to their work. Just so in dance: children can explore the manifold patterns of these particular relationships and give expression to their own ideas and feelings about them. They may dance and meet someone whom they would never normally approach or whirl away from someone who produces in them a real anxiety. Such happenings, occurring within the structure, discipline and freedom of a dance lesson, can be very beneficial experiences.

Lesson 1

Material of the lesson / To explore meeting, parting and staying in groups of three.

GUIDED EXPERIENCE
1. *Start walking to the beat of the drum.*
2. *As you hear changes in the rhythm of the drum beats, respond with different actions, perhaps skip, twirl, patter. But try to keep the rhythm.*
3. *When you hear this sound you should freeze immediately (De-dum.)*
4. *Repeat several times responding to the different drum rhythms— freezing.*

92

DISCOVER   *Now, without the drum . . . make your own sentence of two or three rhythms, and then freeze.*

GUIDED EXPERIENCE   *1. Take a frozen position and when you hear a succession of drum beats gradually reach out towards someone, leading with one open hand or a clenched fist.*
2. When the drum beats stop, hold your position. Make sure that all your attention is concentrated towards the person that your reaching indicates.
3. Repeat: freezing—reaching—holding, several times.

DISCOVER   *Go into twos or threes and find an answer to the following problem:*
a) You start near to each other in a completely frozen group,
b) You leave each other, each one dancing to his own rhythm,
c) You freeze or pause and reach towards each other as though you are reluctant to be apart.
The children should be given time to work on this problem. They will need help in realizing that, because they are each using their own rhythms, they will be stopping at different times. One child may, therefore, have paused and already be reaching towards the others while they are still moving. They should be encouraged to retain this and not give their ideas up for the sake of ease or conformity.

CLARIFY   *Take your starting positions and dance through the sequence against group positions—dance away with own rhythm—pause, reach towards each other and hold.*

94

1. *In your group of three, select one rhythm to which you would all like to move.*
2. *Now use that rhythm to travel together from place to place.*
3. *Use the rhythm, but stay together in one place and keep the rhythm going in parts of your body. You might:*
a) *clap or click, with your hands,*
b) *jump or stamp, with your feet,*
c) *use your body by twisting your spine.*
The children should be given time to explore the possibilities of these three experiences.

Find the answer to the following problems:
1. *You are three or two people moving together and using the same rhythm.*
2. *You pause near to each other and continue with a group rhythm.*
3. *Suddenly you break away, using your own rhythms.*
4. *You pause, reach towards each other, then freeze.*

Once the children have had time to work on the problem, they should finalize their ideas into a definite repeatable movement sequence.

95

NOTES TO THE TEACHER

1. In the first part of the lesson, drum simple rhythms which could accompany skipping, running, stamping; and rhythms of 3/4 or 4/4 time which have an emphasis on any one of the beats.

2. When the children are reaching *towards* each other, encourage them to do so with different body parts, and from different positions. Do not let the word "towards" come to mean solely that the total body is facing the other person.

3. When the children start together in a frozen group, help them to develop the feeling of belonging and relating to each other. This can be helped by the focus of attention, body position, and degree of tension in the body.

4. When the children are dancing away, using their own rhythms, they will need to be given confidence in retaining their own ideas.

5. Draw the attention of the children to the fact that when people are together, they often talk about similar things. The rhythm represents this similar topic and it is the interests of the rhythm which bind them together.

6. Once the children leave each other they become individuals again, each using his own rhythm. When they pause and look towards each other again, this could easily become the beginning of another situation.

7. Try to draw parallels for the children in the dance situation and many everyday situations.

LEADING AND FOLLOWING

It is important for children to learn to be socially acceptable, or their way in life will be made more difficult. So often children will be faced with problems of friends; of one day becoming leaders with the danger of alienating the main group of children. They have to make adjustments which perhaps demand that temporarily they lose the leadership of a group and become a follower. A follower has to be encouraged to find the confidence, motivation and interest that will attract others to him, and so give him temporary leadership. Dance cannot solve many of the day-to-day problems which children encounter, but it can go a long way towards helping them to explore qualities of both leading and following.

In situations of leading and following it is important to help the children to develop not only both of these capacities, but the knowledge of when to change from one role to the other.

Lesson 2

Material of the lesson / To help develop the capacity for leading and following in group situations.

GUIDED EXPERIENCE

1. *Select a group of five and number yourselves one to five.*
2. *Each one of you think of an action from one of the action word columns.* (See page 2.)
3. *As a group decide on a movement symbol which you will use to start one person moving away from your group. You can use a simple jump from two feet to two feet, a double hand clap, a quick group shiver.*
4. *When your group makes the action, Number 1 leaves the group and starts his action. The rest of the group one by one join Number 1 and take up the action. For example: if Number 1 leaves, he may*

97

*decide to start a rising and sinking, turning action. Once Number 2
sees this, he joins Number 1. Then in turn 3, 4, and 5 join in.
5. Once you have all joined in Number 1's action, stop, make your
group action, and off goes Number 2.*

DISCOVER   1. Allow the children plenty of time to practice the above before
setting the next problem.
2. *Find out how you can keep your work going continually until
you have gone from Number 1 to 5 without stopping.*

DISCUSSION   1. *Amongst yourselves, decide which of the actions you were able
to follow clearly and why.*
2. *Decide what were the things that you had to do when you were
one of the group followers.*

GUIDED EXPERIENCE   1. *Form a group of three and create a group shape which is full of
holes.*
2. *Explore changing from one group shape to another but always
make sure you are creating holes.*
3. *Without speaking to each other change the grouping until you
have a solid shape of any kind, i.e., without holes.*
4. *Return to another grouping with holes.*
5. *Without speaking to each other, and with one of you assuming
the role of leader, change to a solid grouping. Keep changing from
one grouping to the other; each time you change from a holed to
a solid group shape, a different person assumes the leading role.*

CLARIFY   *Create three simple group changes, each time showing clearly who
instigates the change.*

NOTES TO THE TEACHER

1. For this lesson the categories of action words should be displayed
on the chalk-board, an overhead projector, or a display card. They
should be easily visible from all parts of the room.
2. The discussion part of this lesson is extremely important and
somewhat more time than usual may be needed for this. During the
discussion, or as a result of it, try to draw out from the children
the following points:

A Leader:

a) must make his actions clear by performing them with confidence,
b) must select something which is challenging and exciting but not
too complicated,
c) must continue his action for a sufficient length of time for others
to see it.

A Follower:

a) must observe carefully the action of the leader,
b) must repeat clearly and accurately the leader's ideas so as not to confuse those following him,
c) must help the leader by a contributing attitude.

SHADOWING

The term shadowing is used for two main reasons: It is a qualitative word which evokes sensitivity of movement, and it can combine within it leading, following and mirroring.

When presented with the task of shadowing, a Grade 4 class immediately grasped the concept and produced some simple but extremely sensitive work. When the concept of shadowing was presented to a Grade 3 class, the magnitude of the problem was too great and they could do nothing with the material. In this case the earlier stages of leading and following, and mirroring had been omitted, and the children were not ready. In Grade 4, although the earlier dance concepts had been omitted, all the other general developmental stages of learning, having had a further year to develop, made it possible for the children to immediately handle the concept. If the children in Grades 4 to 6 are finding it difficult to work with shadowing, then the teacher would need to give some more selective and appropriate work on leading, following and mirroring.

Lesson 3

Material of the lesson / To develop, with a partner, the concept of "shadowing".

DISCUSSION

You have all seen your own shadow. It is made by the sun or a strong light shining on you from an angle. The place of the shadow depends upon the source of the light. You can face your shadow, turn you back on it, or have it at your side. As you move, your shadow moves.

GUIDED EXPERIENCE

1. Find a partner and decide which one of you will be the shadow and who will be the real person.
2. Now the real person turns his shadow into different shapes.

DISCOVER

Find out what happens to your shadow when you do things very quickly and when you do them very slowly.
Perhaps—the shadow finds it very difficult to stay with you when you do things very quickly. The shadow, when you move very quickly, catches the quality of what you do but not exactly how you do it.

99

GUIDED EXPERIENCE   *Work with your shadow again and this time be considerate of him. Sometimes make it very clear exactly the kind of movement you are using. At other times, show clearly the quality of what you are doing. For example, you may be clearly moving into an angular shape and then equally clearly skipping or bouncing in a gay manner.*

CLARIFY   *Now you have some ideas to work with, make a short dance called "My Shadow". Repeat it until you really know it, how it starts, what happens and how it ends.*
Once the children have completed this short dance, explore another idea with shadows.

DISCUSSION   *We discussed earlier that your shadow depends upon the angle of light hitting you. What happens when the sun moves and is directly above you? Your shadow disappears. This time we will create a dance called "The Disappearing Shadow".*

Dance with your shadow but then let one of these things happen:
a) You dance from one place to another and gradually your shadow gets left behind,
b) You dance in one place very close to your shadow and gradually your shadow sinks to the floor,
c) You dance in one place and gradually your shadow leaves you and goes farther and farther away.

Once the children have had time and help working on this idea the lesson could be brought to a close with either dance.

Decide which dance you will now perform, "The Shadow" or "The Disappearing Shadow".

NOTES TO THE TEACHER

1. The children should be given the opportunity of both being the shadow and producing the shadow. The change over in roles may be left to the children or directed by the teacher. It is important that children stay with one part a sufficient length of time to permit them to feel the learning experience involved. The teacher should be aware that the children require different lengths of time to absorb the learning process.

2. When dancing "The Disappearing Shadow", the children should be developing the ability to respond to their partner in a contradictory way. When the child is bouncing or jumping on the spot and the shadow has to gradually sink or fade away the movement situation is a conflicting one. The shadow has to have the intellectual and emotional ability to produce the opposite action. The children may need considerable help with this part of the dance.

FURTHER IDEAS FOR DEVELOPING COMPLETE OR PARTIAL SHADOWING

Grade IV

The Jig-Saw Puzzle

Task One

With partners 'A' and 'B'. 'A' travels and creates a shape which represents the missing part of the puzzle. 'B' travels and fills the missing part by producing the identical shape.

Task Two

'A' cuts the outline of the missing shape in the air. 'B' cuts the same outline in the air. 'A' and 'B' together make the shape of the missing piece.

101

Task Three

'A' and 'B' together cut the outline of the missing shape on the floor.

Machinery

Task One

'A' and 'B' together create a piston-like action, they may do this working in unison or in opposition. The shape and rhythm should be the same.

Task Two

'A' and 'B' together create a circular action. Again the action may be in unison or in opposition. The shape and rhythm should be the same.

Task Three

'A' and 'B' travel together with a bouncing action and pass through a machine which cuts them into identical shapes. After holding their shape for several bounces they revert to normal and pass through the machine again.

Task Four

Three pairs join together and create their own dance "Machinery" from Tasks 1, 2, and 3.

Grades V and VI

Egyptian Frieze

Task One

In twos, walking to a steady 4/4 beat, the body position held on top of the walk is changed every fourth beat. The body position for the two must be identical.

Task Two

In twos, maintaining an identical position of the body, change the pattern of locomotion every eight beats. For example, walk for eight, jump feet astride for eight, hop for eight.

Task Three

Using the upper half of the body as a base, change leg positions in the air on every fourth beat.

Task Four

Using a rhythmical 4/4 beat as background music, create a frieze which uses in sequence Tasks 1, 2 and 3.

ACTION AND RESPONSE, OR CONVERSATION IN MOVEMENT

The word "conversation" implies a give and take of ideas on a similar topic. The conversation may be one in which agreement predominates or, conversely, the topic may be fiercely argued. The conversationalists may politely wait their turn to speak or may, in their haste or excitement, overlap their statements. At times conversation becomes so heated that everybody is speaking at once.

Conversation in dance is developed on very similar lines. 'A' moves, 'B' moves, 'A' and 'B' overlap their moving. 'A' and 'B' both move at the same time. Responding to a partner in dance requires acute observation in the same way that responding in speech requires listening. A good conversationalist acquires the art through both sensitivity and practice. Similarly a good conversationalist in movement will need to develop sensitivity and practice in his art. Shadowing has started the children on the way to speaking together in movement.

Mastering the art of conversation in movement makes it possible for things to happen. Certainly dance can be accomplished alone, but a much wider field of communication and expression is opened up once the children can move with each other in the give and take of a corporate idea. Conversation in movement is particularly aimed at developing the ability of give and take.

Normal conversation usually centers around a topic, which is its content. In dance, conversation in movement also has content. The content could derive from any of the areas we have studied: from body, effort or space; from "idea" such as "The clowns"; from responding to a particular piece of music, or the quality of the percussion instruments; or finally a mood such as "freedom" or "power". In Grade 6, in particular, the children are often concerned with such important issues as heroism, power, trust, peace, pollution. This struggle to understand the concrete issues of the world and to search for the real meaning of concepts of loyalty, beauty, or democracy often form starting points for their dance, and fulfil an important need for the children.

These ideas can be translated into movement terms by the teacher. The presentation of the idea is then given to the children at a level at which they can understand it. These presentations can stimulate a response which is profound and are important for that reason. The following lesson on "Freedom" and "Bondage" is translated into a simple movement problem in partner conversation.

Lesson 4

Material of the lesson / To work with a partner in a situation which demands moving and responding. The movement to convey the expression of "Bondage and Freedom".
(Using a chalkboard or cards:)

GUIDED EXPERIENCE

Select one of these two columns of action words and join the words together in an action sequence:

Rising	*Running*
Sinking	*Jumping*
Shrinking	*Turning*
Rolling	*Rising*

DISCOVER

Which sentence of actions seems to connect in mood with which of the two columns of words below?

Bound	*Free*
Imprisoned	*Open*
Enclosed	*Lighthearted*
Struggling	

CLARIFY

Go through your sentence again but this time, bring out very clearly which idea you are portraying: The idea of being "bound" or "free".

GUIDED EXPERIENCE

With a partner develop the following idea. 'A' is free, 'B' is bound. You speak to each other, in movement, telling each other about your freedom and your imprisonment. One speaks and then the other speaks.

CLARIFY

Allow the children time to work on this idea and encourage them not to make their sentences too long.

GUIDED EXPERIENCE

One of you is now going to influence your partner to join you in either your freedom or imprisonment.

CLARIFY

Once the children have developed this part they should clarify the complete sequence, of 'A' speaking, and 'B' speaking, and both speaking of the same idea.

FURTHER IDEAS FOR DEVELOPING
CONVERSATION WITH A PARTNER

"Talking Percussion"

Task One

Each partner selects a percussion instrument and works out a short sequence with his instrument.

Task Two

The partners meet each other at the end of their sequence.

Task Three

They speak to each other with their percussion ending with either a violent quarrel or in total agreement.

"Strange Meeting"

Task One

Each partner selects a characteristic movement sequence made from two effort actions. 'A' might be a "flicker" and "puncher", 'B' a "floater" and "slasher".

Task Two

The partners meet and again a conversation is carried on about their respective characteristics.

Task Three

The situation is resolved by each going his own way.

"Copycat"

Task One

A simple follow-the-leader situation is set using either actions or shapes as the main leading theme.

Task Two

The partners have to develop a sense of timing which makes the sequence a conversation rather than simple follow the leader:
'A' moves—pause
'B' copies—pause

'A' moves, 'B' *immediately* copies
'A' moves—long pause
'B' moves—long pause
Finish

Task Three

The children clarify exactly what happens during the pause. Do they simply stop and look at each other? Do they put in any other actions to show their mood?

RELATING TO GROUP QUALITY AND DYNAMICS

The dynamics of a group can also express mood and emotions. For example a group using all quick actions might suggest a mood of excitement, irritation, or fun. Children react more quickly to mood and emotion than do adults. A mood can run through a group of children as quickly as the wind stirs the still grass. In group dance it is possible to capture this contagious effect which movement has for children, and through their interest, bring about spontaneous and formed group dances. When working in dance, it is conceivable that the idea being danced out may need to have an emotion portrayed by a group. It is extremely difficult for any other than the most skillful and mature to produce, out of nowhere, a mood of sadness. On the other hand guidance in using certain actions, such as sinking and closing, can help to bring about an expression of sadness. In most instances in children's dance, mood should be arrived at through action, not action through mood. Work in group dynamics should, therefore, be work based upon the time, energy, space factors. These may result solely in group action, or may produce group action plus mood and emotion. Both should be acceptable.

RELATING TO GROUP SHAPE

To relate to a group shape it is necessary to be able to observe the shape, the tensions, and the feeling which are being conveyed. From this it is also necessary to be able to adjust, add, harmonize and increase the total group expression. Every child within the group should be sensing the importance of being a small but totally necessary part of a functioning structure. The function, in this instance, being to convey a certain group shape. The fundamental

107

group shapes are outlined in Chapter 5 and these simple forms can provide the group work.

There are several approaches which can be used:

a) A child starts a group shape by clearly indicating a form which is rounded, curved, plastic, arrow-shape or block-shape. Several children in turn add to the original shape, trying at the same time to retain the original ideas.

b) The children, in small groups, create one of the shapes. Simultaneously, they move to change their group shape into another different but identifiable one.

c) On hearing the drum beaten they spontaneously create groups of different sizes, each group having an identifiable shape. For example, one group of three children may be arrow-shaped whilst another of eight is twisted. This has a play-like element in it which the children find both stimulating and enjoyable. At the same time it helps them to make quick observations, assessments and reactions to each other.

Creating group shapes can be regarded as one of the simplest forms of group work. It is not difficult for children. It is, however, important for them to develop a *feeling* for group shape and not just for *making* shapes. The former requires total involvement, concentration and sensitivity. A sculptor would bring these three factors to bear upon the creation of one of his works. So too must the children be helped to develop these attitudes towards their work if it is to be a sincere and meaningful experience.

RELATING TO GROUP TOUCH

Many aspects of group work can be developed without touch being used. The point arrives, however, when it will be necessary for the children to use their sense of touch in creating group work. This has certain problems for children during these three years. They relate in particular to their social and emotional development. Children as early as Grade 4 are already showing a strong preference for working with their own sex. By Grades 5 and 6 it is often very difficult for the children to accept any form of mixed group work. Both the children and dance lose a great deal if this situation is allowed to persist but any change can only be brought about slowly and sensitively by the teacher. Group work which requires using touch has to be developed within this already established framework of social behaviour.

Emotionally, some children will dislike the gripping, pulling, pushing, linking, balancing activities, which are a part of group work. They will react against the sensation and consequent emotion which is aroused when a group is required to be in close contact.

Physically, boys may appear to enjoy the rough and tumble of some contact activities, whereas the girls shun away from them. These are a few of the problems, but they can be counterbalanced by the care with which the teacher presents the material.

Simple objective movement problems can be gradually introduced: In a group of three, create a mobile which is held together by the finest wire. Create a strongly linked chain. These two situations are objective, non-emotional yet require two different forms of touch, the very delicate and the very strong.

In circles, lines, blocks, children can create rising, sinking, opening, closing, advancing, retreating, and travelling groups, linked by varying strengths of touch from finger tips, elbows, shoulders and hands. As in conversation they have to assume the responsibility for speaking, hearing, accepting, passing on, changing. Instead of words being their medium for communication, they are using movement.

Lessons in Group Work

When group work is introduced in any of the years from nine to twelve, children will be at different stages in their understanding, interest, motivation, and abilities, in dance. If the children are at the appropriate stage they can be encouraged to explore many pure movement problems. They may be ready to work solely on group movement problems, enjoying them for their own sake. For example, a group might explore lightly touching the floor with their feet; travelling together retaining the light touch on the floor; lightly making contact with each other by touching and together sink to the floor. Another group might explore touching the floor lightly with finger tips; together whirling and then lightly joining together as a group, again using the finger tips.

They may, on the other hand, be at the stage where the pure movement problems have little or no appeal for them. In this case group work can be handled by exciting the imagination. Rocks that have been imbedded in the earth for thousands of years are suddenly split by dynamite. Bristles on a paint brush take on their own life and decorate the room. Interpreting legend and history, capturing the actions, moods and qualities in verse or prose, all lead to experience in group work.

For the purpose of illustrating what can occur in group work, the legend of "Point Grey" has been developed. The latter part of the legend of "Point Grey" is given as it occurs in the book *Legends of Vancouver* by E. Pauline Johnson. Then from this legend certain of the main features are developed into a simple dance-drama. The lessons will be structured to involve the children in all the aforementioned aspects of group work and will indicate a possible approach for using stimuli other than pure movement for group work.

It was not always there, that great rock, drawing its strength and its wonderful power from the seas, for it, too, was once a Great Tyee, who ruled a mighty tract of waters. He was god of all the waters that wash the coast, of the Gulf of Georgia, of Puget Sound, of the Straits of Juan de Fuca, of the waters that beat against even the west coast to Vancouver Island, and of all the channels that cut between the Charlotte Islands. He was Tyee of the West Wind, and his storms and tempests were so mighty that the Sagalie Tyee Himself could not control the havoc that he created. He warred upon all fishing craft, he demolished canoes and sent men to graves in the sea. He uprooted forests and drove the surf on shore heavy with wreckage of despoiled trees and with beaten and bruised fish. He did all this to reveal his powers, for he was cruel and hard of heart, and he would laugh and defy the Sagalie Tyee, and looking up to the sky he would call, "See how powerful I am, how mighty how strong; I am as great as you."

It was at this time that the Sagalie Tyee in the persons of the Four Men came in the great canoe up over the rim of the Pacific, in the age thousands of years ago when they turned the evil into stone, and the kindly into trees.

"Now," said the god of the West Wind, "I can show how great I am. I shall blow a tempest that these men may not land on my coast. They shall not ride by seas and sounds and channels in safety. I shall wreck them and send their bodies into the great deeps, and I shall be Sagalie Tyee in their place and ruler of all the world." So the god of the West Wind blew forth his tempests. The waves arose mountain high, the seas lashed and thundered along the shores. The roar of his mighty breath could be heard wrenching giant limbs from the forest trees, whistling down the canyons and dealing death and destruction for leagues and leagues along the coast. But the canoe containing the Four Men rode upright through all the heights and hollows of the seething ocean. No curling crest or sullen depth could wreck that magic craft, for the hearts it bore were filled with kindness for the human race, and kindness cannot die.

It was all rock and dense forest, and unpeopled; only wild animals and sea birds sought the shelter it provided from the terrors of the West Wind; but he drove them out in sullen anger, and made on this strip of land his last stand against the Four Men. The Paleface calls the place Point Grey, but the Indians yet speak of it as "The Battle Ground of the West Wind." All his mighty forces he now brought to bear against the oncoming canoe; he swept great hurricanes about the stony ledges; he caused the sea to beat and swirl in tempestuous fury along its narrow fastnesses, but the canoe came nearer and nearer, invincible as those shores, and stronger than death itself. As the bow touched the land the Four Men arose and commanded the West Wind to cease his war cry and mighty though he had been, his voice trembled and sobbed itself into a gentle breeze, then fell to a whispering note, then faded into exquisite silence.

110

"Oh, you evil one with the unkind heart," cried the Four Men, "you have been too great a god for even the Sagalie Tyee to obliterate you forever, but you shall turn into stone where you now stand, and you shall rise only as men wish you to. Your life from this day shall be for the good of man, for when the fisherman's sails are idle and his lodge is leagues away you shall fill those sails and blow his craft free, in whatever direction he desires. You shall stand where you are through all the thousands upon thousands of years to come, and he who touches you with his paddle blade shall have his desire of a breeze to carry him home."

The following group work will be necessary for developing the dance-drama:
1. The great Tyee of the West Wind: he creates storms and tempests.
2. The sea, forests, fish, and birds who were affected by the tempests of the West Wind.
3. The Sagalie Tyee who came in the person of Four Men in a great canoe.
The episodes which can be developed are:
1. The arrival of the Great Tyee and the creating of the raging storm.
2. The coming of the Four Men in the canoe.
3. The battle for power between the Great Tyee and the Four Men.
4. The subduing and turning to rock of the Great Tyee.

DEVELOPMENT

Before commencing work in the dance lessons the children should have read the legend and been given opportunity for discussing how it could be developed in dance. In this way they will be prepared for the following movement experiences.

Lesson 1

Material of the lesson / The arrival of the Great Tyee and the creating of the raging storm.

GUIDED EXPERIENCE

1. *In order to depict the Great Tyee we will have three people working together. By using three people together we can increase the feeling of power and strength which the Great Tyee would have.*
2. *Find a group of three and start working on leaping actions which have very strong, powerful shapes in the air.*
3. *Once you have found your own shape, decide on the rhythm in which you can leap together. This might be run—leap—run—leap;*

or leap, leap, leap, freeze. Practice until you are really a group of three who move together to the same rhythm.

DISCOVER   *Go to the sides of the room and find out how many times you need to repeat your leaping sentence to bring you in to the center of the room.*

FORMULATE   *1. These simple but powerful and rhythmical leaps create the character of the Great Tyee as he enters the scene. Practice once more, in your threes, and really project this feeling.*
2. Once you feel you have arrived and have control of the world, freeze your group action into stillness.
Allow the children time for completing this part before proceeding.

GUIDED EXPERIENCE   *Now let us work on group ideas which will represent the elements of the sea: fish, birds, waves, seaweed.*
1. Break away from your three and find a space.
2. When you hear the drum, run very quickly in many directions, one direction after the other.
3. When you hear a double beat on the drum immediately join with some others. As you join, link together by touching with some body part.
4. Stay with this new group.
5. Keeping linked together try these two ideas:
a) travelling with any action,
b) rising and sinking.
Allow the children time to explore this form of group work. Encourage them when necessary to keep in contact, to have a light touch, to be aware of the others in the group.
6. Using either travelling, rising and sinking, or a sequence of both activities, start very slowly but gradually build the tempo until you are moving very quickly.
7. Increase the tempo to such a degree that you are forced to break away from your group. Move away from your group and freeze at any level.

CLARIFY   *Rejoin your group and clarify your idea of rising and sinking, travelling—increasing tempo—break—freeze.*

FORMULATE   The teacher should now help the children to create the first part of the legend, the arrival of the Great Tyee and the creating of the storm. The following suggestions are designed to help the teachers. However, they may find they have their own ideas which they wish to develop.
1. One or two groups of three represent the Great Tyee. These groups wait at the sides or corners of the room.
2. The other groups are frozen in varying places about the room.

They represent the sea, birds, fish and elements of the ocean.

3. The Great Tyee, using the previously developed motifs, enters. Gradually the Great Tyee increases the power of his actions. The groups start to move and then the storm breaks.

4. Gradually or suddenly everything stops.

5. At this point the Four Men in the canoe will enter. The movement ideas for this one are developed in the following lesson.

Lesson 2

PART I

GUIDED EXPERIENCE

Material of the lesson / The entering of the Four Men in the canoe.

1. *Find a space and try the following step pattern: step deep then lift onto the toes and take three small steps.*

2. *Keep your body very upright as you make this step pattern. At the same time focus into the distance.*

3. *If you stepped deep with your right foot, change and step deep with your left foot. In this way the rhythm is accented on the other side of the body.*

DISCOVER

Go into a group of four and see if keeping one behind the other you can keep the rhythm going.

Allow time for the children to develop this before proceeding.

GUIDED EXPERIENCE

1. *Grip your hands.*

2. *Push and pull your gripped hands towards and away from your body.*

3. *Now create a rhythm which has a strong pulling action on beat one. Release or push away on beat two, three and four.*

4. *Once you have got that rhythm, make the action of the arms cut the space on the right or left side of your body.*

5. *Put together the stepping rhythm with the pushing and pulling rhythm. On the deep step you pull, on the high steps you push or release.*

DISCOVER

Go back to your groups and try to keep all of the rhythms going together. You should still be in line one behind the other.

Many of the children will find they can combine both of these actions. If groups find this too difficult, allow them to choose either the stepping or the arm action. If they choose only the arm action, they should try travelling with a simple walking action.

PART II

FORMULATE

The teacher should now put together this lesson with Part One.

1. The canoeists can either enter when the storm is at its height,

113

and then cause the storm to subside, or, they can enter after the storm has subsided.

2. As the canoeists pass each group, it should react, advancing towards, away from, and surrounding the canoe.

3. The Four Men in the canoe continue through all the groups until they safely reach a certain spot.

4. When they reach the spot they simultaneously reach out and touch the land.

5. Everything ceases to move except the Great Tyee. The trios, involved in this, gradually force themselves into a solid "rock-like" group and everything is still.

It will be necessary to take this skeleton outline and develop it further. Time should be spent on helping the groups to react to the Four Men in the canoe. The part which the Great Tyee plays at this point will need to be clarified. Throughout the whole dance the children should be helped to bring out the rhythm and dynamics in the canoeists actions; the feeling of sensitivity to touch in the groups working on the elements in the storm; the feeling for group shape, in the trio portraying the Great Tyee.

The teacher of dance knows that, by observing the children, they enrich her with many ideas. These ideas on developing group relationship are but beginning ones. From observing the many facets of relationship which the children bring out in these and other ideas, the teacher will gain insight into many more which could be developed.

REFERENCES

Johnson, Pauline E. *Legends of Vancouver*. Canada: McClelland and Stewart Limited, 1961.

Lofthouse, Peter. *Dance*. London: Heinemann Educational Books Ltd., 1970.

5

AN ANALYSIS OF LESSON MATERIAL

The foregoing chapters have shown the application of many of the movement concepts which form part of the structure of the creative dance program. They have also indicated a method of approach which is aimed at fostering original and creative thinking. This chapter will consider, in detail, the body of knowledge which forms the basis of the dance program. In creative dance, there is a structure of knowledge which must be understood by both the teacher and the children. It is this structure which allows for the continuous development of movement ideas, as one movement concept leads to another. Ausubel states that you cannot teach creative thinking and critical thinking outside of the context of a specific discipline. He believes that such thinking can only be attained by:

> . . . adopting a precise, logical, analytical, and critical approach to the teaching of a particular discipline, an approach which fosters appreciation of the scientific method in that discipline.[1]

Creative and critical thinking should consequently be one of the outcomes which can be achieved from studying the structure of the body of knowledge of dance.

The structure of knowledge in creative dance, as with other subjects, can only be learned by the children when they are at the required stage of readiness. The following material outlines the aspects of the creative dance structure which, normally, could be acquired by children between the ages of nine and twelve years.

This material can be divided for the purpose of study into four main areas: the body, the effort, the space, and the relationships.

The body itself, which by the nature of its skeletal and muscular structure can be made to move in certain ways.

The effort which occurs whenever action takes place and can be noted as the time, energy, space and flow of movement.

The space which the mass of the body fills and into which all action must go.

[1]John P. DeCecco, *The Psychology of Learning and Instruction* (New Jersey: Prentice-Hall, Inc., 1968), p. 473.

The relationship that occurs between two or more people as their actions interrelate.

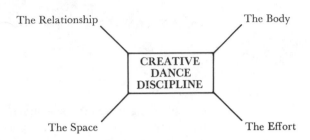

Diagram 1

By continual practical study of the four areas, the children acquire a body of knowledge about movement. From this information the children can be guided: to select the movement material they desire for their dance; to order and form this material into the desired expression and composition; and finally, through the actual practice and performance of the dance, to acquire further physical mastery and understanding of movement concepts.

It is absolutely essential for teachers to appreciate that the four major movement areas are continually interwoven into a total whole, although, for ease of reference, they will now be separated.

THE BODY

Body Functions
The body will bend, stretch and twist.

BEND
When the extremities of the body are brought towards each other either those extremities or the whole body will bend.

STRETCH
When the extremities of the body are pulled away from the center of the body or from one another, the body or its parts will stretch or extend.

TWIST
When some form of rotation takes place and parts of the body turn or rotate away from each other, a twist will occur.

Some form of bending, stretching and twisting is likely to occur

116

in parts of the body during the performance of any action. It is because of the somewhat automatic mechanical and stereotype movements which arise from these words that they should be used with care. A far more creative and qualitative result will arise from using action words.

Body Actions

RUN, SKIP, CREEP RUSH, SLITHER, HOP, GALLOP, DART, FLEE

Travelling Actions / All of these actions take the children from one place to another. The emphasis is on the *going* of the action.

SHIVER, SHAKE, WOBBLE, QUIVER, TREMBLE, PATTER, SHUDDER

Vibratory Actions / These actions demand a very quick *repetitive* movement which may have varying degrees of tensions. They can be performed by parts of the body or the whole body.

LEAP, HURL, TOSS BOUND, PRANCE, BOUNCE, SOAR, FLY

Jumping Actions / The essence of these actions is *elevation* or going upwards and there is a loss of contact with the ground.

SPIN, WHIRL, TWIRL, WHIP, SWIVEL, PIVOT, ROLL

Turning Actions / All of these actions *rotate* the body around an axis.

FREEZE, HOLD, PERCH, GRIP, ANCHOR, PAUSE, SETTLE

Stopping Actions / All *stillness* should have a definite quality and each of these actions will bring this about.

STAMP, PUNCH, EXPLODE, POUND, ERUPT

Percussive Actions / All of these actions are very *explosive,* strong and sudden in quality, and may be performed by the whole body or body parts.

SHRINK, SHRIVEL, CLOSE, SURROUND, CLASP

Contracting Actions / All of these actions make the body and its parts *smaller* than normal. They will also generally close towards a central focus.

GROW, EXPAND, RELEASE, OPEN

Expanding Actions / All of these actions move *outward* from a central point and the body may extend beyond its normal range of openness.

COLLAPSE, SINK, LOWER, DRIP, DROP

Sinking Actions / All of these actions move in a *downward* direction.

LIFT, RISE, SUSPEND

Rising Actions / All of these move in an *upward* direction.

REACH, APPROACH

Advancing Actions / These actions move *forwards* in space.

RECOIL, WITHDRAW

Retreating Actions / These actions move *backwards* in space.

These action words cover many aspects of movement: activity, quality, and space are the foundation stones of creative dance. Each

word will have a different movement sensation, feeling, quality and expression. The number of words, consequently, gives the children a wide range of movement upon which to draw when interpreting their ideas into dance.

Body parts / Body joints

HEAD, ARMS, HANDS,
TRUNK, LEGS, FEET,
ELBOWS, WRISTS, KNEES,
ANKLES, SHOULDERS

In differentiating between body parts and joints, children learn to use their bodies with exactness.

The whole-body actions are normally spontaneous movements, but once attention is given to bodily organization—what each part of the body is doing—a skilled and educated use of the body is being developed. These parts and joints can be used in the following ways:

a) to come together separately or as a whole,
b) to extend away from each other separately or as a whole,
c) to pass each other by,
d) to work together in contact,
e) to work together but not in contact,
f) to lead the main actions,
g) to combine various aspects of the above points.

Body Zones

RIGHT SIDE
LEFT SIDE
FRONT HALF
BACK HALF
UPPER HALF
LOWER HALF

The skeletal system divides the body naturally into these normal zones. Children at first move with their bodies placed in the normal zones. Later, they learn to use areas of the body in different zones. For example, the right side moves over to the left, the upper to the lower, and the upper left to the lower right. The least used zone is the back area of the body.

It is through being able to locate their bodies in other zones that children learn to to balance their bodies, to produce co-ordinated movements, and to develop an awareness of where they are in space—all are vital components of everyday movement.

Body Shape

CURLED OR ROUNDED
ANGULAR OR TWISTED
EXTENDED—WALL SHAPED
EXTENDED—ARROW SHAPED

These four shapes can be identified in movement. Sometimes the body will make one clearly defined shape, but frequently there will be an interplay of many shapes. The shape of the body can be felt most clearly when a position is maintained. Following upon that, it is possible to feel the shape of the body in any of the jumping actions when again the body is held in stillness in flight. Finally,

120

the children can develop a continuing awareness of the shape of their body when they are in motion.

Body Symmetry and Asymmetry

SYMMETRY   The body is normally balanced in both shape and size, one side being identical to the other. This knowledge grows out of an awareness of body shape. The body is divided into two halves by the spine. Each side can be identical in shape and action or one side can differ from the other. Although at this stage children would find it extremely difficult to create dances using symmetry and asymmetry, they should be introduced to both the term and the concept. Symmetry is balanced and the positions tend to be very stable and the actions restricted.

ASYMMETRY   The body is asymmetrical when its two sides are moved or placed into a contrasting situation. The majority of actions are asymmetrical and this produces flexible and fluid movements. Asymmetry has a greater sensation of going in movement.

Body Base

All action starts from a position, be this on the feet, the seat, the knees, or the trunk. Children can be helped to become interested and aware of where their dance starts, pauses, ends, by being given the opportunity to explore these different bases. As with body shape some of the positions explored may include more than one aspect. However, awareness of the possibilities of starting positions increases total awareness.

STANDING   Any position of the body where the weight is supported by the feet. This may be with two feet or one foot, in an extended, or a contracted position.

SITTING   Any position of the body where the weight is supported by the seat. If other parts of the body are touching the floor, e.g., the hands, they are there to enhance the shape or position rather than to support the weight of the body.

KNEELING   Any position of the body where the weight is taken on one or both knees.

LYING   Any position of the body where the weight is taken on the trunk. This may be on the back, side, or front, and the body may be curled or extended.

121

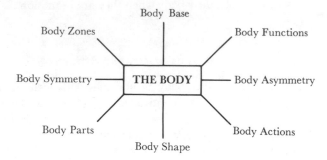

Diagram 2

The above material on the body indicates what should be covered during these years. Different areas will be studied at different levels of understanding and teachers will find that children enjoy some areas more than others. However, constant reference to these areas will ensure that the children are given a balanced program in this material.

THE EFFORT

As indicated in Chapter 2, the quality or texture of movement is produced not by the action but by the attitudes towards time, energy, and space which are displayed through the action. As a young child comes to greet you, his action may be running. What you see and record is not the actual running but the quality of the action, the sensation which it conveys. You respond to the quality of the action rather than the action. In the structure of creative dance children learn to recognize certain qualities which can be differentiated from others in the same way as they learn that round can be differentiated from square, and blue from red. The word "effort" encompasses this recognition of different qualities within an action.

Time
This does not refer to the linear effect of time as seconds, minutes, and hours pass by; but to the attitude towards time that can be seen in an action.

SUDDEN Here the attitude is one of time contracting, of urgency, haste, attention, alertness, of everything inside ticking over very rapidly.

122

The action associated with this attitude will also be rapid. The force of the action may be strong or light. It may be one of great suddenness followed by a pause, or a succession of rapid smaller actions within a larger one.

SUSTAINED   The sensation and attitude of sustainment has the effect of enduring, never-ending. The actions which are associated with this attitude will be actions which are elongated in time and are performed with a drawing-out of the action. This does not mean the size of the action has to be increased, but the length of time in which it is performed is drawn out.

It is inevitable that a sustained action will take longer to perform than a sudden action—as a stop-watch will verify. It is not enough just to ask the children to move slowly. Externally, they may have moved slowly and yet not have experienced the sensation of sustainment. As a teacher, you are working towards helping the children feel the sensation and the attitude, and are not concerned with the external time in seconds and minutes.

Energy

Every action is performed with a certain degree of muscular tension which could be recorded in terms of pounds and ounces by the correct measuring instruments. In dance, one is not concerned with this external measurement of energy but with an attitude towards this tension. The sensation of producing energy gives the children the opportunity of developing an awareness and sensitivity toward their own ability to produce internal changes of energy.

FIRMNESS   An attitude towards energy which will produce a strong action and contains considerable muscular tension.

FINETOUCH   An attitude towards energy which will produce a very light, delicate action and contains a fine degree of muscular tension.

Combinations of Time and Energy

The two factors sudden and sustained, can be combined with the two factors of energy, firmness and finetouch. When these combinations are made the attitude towards time and energy will produce actions which are sudden and strong, sudden and finetouch, sustained and strong, sustained and finetouch. Changing between these qualities in actions not only demands considerable physical skill but heightens the awareness of attitude.

SUSTAINED—FINETOUCH   These actions will be delicate in strength and lingering in time.

SUSTAINED—FIRM   These actions will be lingering in time but powerful in strength.

SUDDEN—FINETOUCH   These actions will be delicate in strength but hastening in time.

SUDDEN—FIRM   These actions will be powerful in strength but hastening in time.

123

For further descriptions of action words and qualities relating to the time—energy factors, reference should be made to Chapter 2.

Space

Actions move through space in both a direct, concentrated way and a flexible, pliant way. The tendency toawrds directness or flexibility in an action by a child is often a byproduct of his attitude towards the spatial factor of movement. Some children will have an attitude towards space which is contained and direct and this can be seen by the way in which they approach everyday activities. Others will have a flexible, pliant attitude, again evidenced in their activities. And still others will not have a strong preference and will interchange a great deal between the two. The two factors are referred to as the spatial attitude which is present in any action.

FLEXIBLE   These actions will be flexible, roundabout, pliable, plastic in nature.

DIRECT   These actions will be concentrated, focused, direct, undeviating in nature.

Time-Energy-Space Combinations

Attitudes towards space can be combined with attitudes towards time and energy and produce what are referred to as the *Effort Actions*. These effort actions were formulated by Rudolf Laban and have made a significant contribution towards the educational theory of creative dance.

EFFORT ACTIONS

Sustained + Finetouch + Direct = Glide
Actions which delicately and slowly cut through space. They produce the sensations of gentleness, precision, smoothness.

Sustained + Finetouch + Flexible = Float
Actions which have plasticity and meander gently through space. They produce the sensations of dreaminess, drifting.

Sustained + Strong + Flexible = Wring
Actions which have strength and plisticity as they move slowly through space. They have the sensation of writhing, and wrestling.

Sustained + Strong + Direct = Press
Actions which have strength and directness as they move slowly through space. They have the sensation of force, power, concentration.

Sudden + Finetouch + Direct = Dab
Actions which "pat" the air or an object quickly yet with lightness

and directness. They have the sensation of immediately, pecking, tapping.

Sudden + Finetouch + Flexible = Flick
Actions which quickly and lightly weave through the air. They have the sensation of flickering, fluttering, excitement, fun.

Sudden + Strong + Direct = Punch
Actions which move rapidly with strength and directness. They have the sensation of hammering, hitting, power, determination.

Sudden + Strong + Flexible = Slash
Actions which move rapidly with strength and flexibility. They have the sensation of disturbing, whipping, erupting.

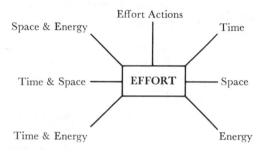

Diagram 3

Children between the ages of nine and twelve are both interested in and capable of producing the several effort actions in answer to many simple movement problems. These children are able to distinguish between direct opposites such as punch and float; but the more complex work of gradual transition, knowledge of the effort cube, and effort and shape, will need to be left for later years.

SPACE

All action cuts a pattern in space. A pattern occurs on the floor when we walk or run, in the air as we gesture with our arms and hands. The shape of our body outlines a pattern in space as we sit or kneel. Our eyes connect us to parts in space with invisible lines. So in everyday activities we are using space, consciously or unconsciously, selecting and ordering our movements into spatial sequences which may be efficient, inefficient, creative, stereotyped, original or reflex patterns. Artists, writers, architects, consciously use and manipulate space to achieve a required effect, be this functional or artistic. Creative dance also requires knowledge and discipline of how to consciously use space to enhance or create. Children's spatial awareness can be awakened and heightened in the same way as their eyes can be opened to the disciplines and beauties of nature, art, and poetry. To do this it is necessary to study the structure of space and form as it can be developed during these years.

Extensions

The size of any action does not need to be uniform. Changes in the size of an action occur when the extensions in space, which are being used, vary.

LARGE OR FAR FROM THE BODY CENTER — These actions are expansive and extend far into the space surrounding the body.

SMALL OR NEAR TO THE BODY CENTER — These actions are confined and stay near to the body center using only that space closely surrounding the body.

Directions

FROM THE CENTER OF THE BODY — Directions are movements outward from the center of the body at different angles, some being more common than others. All the directions outward should be used, including the six fundamental ones, of forward, backwards up, down and to the left or right. The actions may be of simple looking, or of gesturing outward into space in many directions.

TO THE CENTER OF THE BODY — As directions radiate outwards they also converge inwards. Conscious awareness should be developed of the way in which movements use directions as they come back into the body center.

Levels

Levels will usually change when positions are changed from standing to sitting, to kneeling and lying. Levels, high, medium and deep, refer to the way in which an action is being performed in relation to space. This will also occur when performing actions of leaping and jumping. When it is left in a normal position the body will be at a medium level as in actions of walking, running, skipping, and when allowing it to sink it will be deep, as in all sinking, rolling actions.

HIGH
MEDIUM
DEEP

Floor Patterns

These are external to the child because they are created outside of the body. Their design can however have a considerable effect upon the nature of the dance.

126

ZIG ZAG OR ANGULAR PATTERN	Here the stress is upon the corners and the angularity of the pattern.
CURVING OR OPEN CURVE	Here the stress is upon the rounded, sweeping nature of the line.
CIRCLE OR CLOSED CURVE	Here the stress is upon the unbroken essence of a circle.
STRAIGHT LINE	Here the stress is upon the linear directness of going from A to B.

Air Patterns

Again the air patterns are external to the children, being created around them or left by them as they move through space. These can be identified in a similar way to floor patterns but have the added advantage of being three-dimensional.

Focus

When all of the senses are concentrated upon one thing we are giving it our full attention. In dance we can concentrate this attention into one direction and bring a focus of attention to that spot. This creates a visual tension between the child and the focus which is outside of him and so gives clarity of expression to the movement.

Space Words

OVER, UNDER, NEAR, FAR, ABOVE, BELOW, BETWEEN, BESIDE, AROUND

These words should be explored alone, and with other people (above or below a partner, one group near to another group), or in an imaginative situation where through action they portray the idea of being between, under, beside.

Basic Spatial Actions

RISING
This action lifts the body or a body part from one position upward in space to another position. The feeling, sensation and concentration is upon the space through which the body is rising and upon the focus towards which the action is moving.

SINKING
The action lowers the body or a body part from one position downward in space to another position. Again the concern of the mover is with the sinking away from general space.

ADVANCING
The action moves the body or a body part *forward* through space. The movement may be small or extensive but the feeling of the action is forward, advancing through space.

RETREATING
The action draws the body or a body part backwards through space. The feeling is of pulling backwards or stepping backwards away from general space.

127

OPENING   This action *spreads* the body or a body part away from its center. The feeling sensation and concentration is upon opening, spreading into space.

CLOSING   The action *shuts* the body or a body part away from space and encloses it around its own center. During the closing action the sensation, feeling and concentration is upon the closing away from general space.

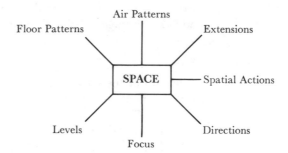

Diagram 4

In working with space the teacher must be constantly aware of the intellectual demands which projecting outside of action into an awareness of particular spaces makes on children. Considerable time should be allowed for this development to take place and practice given on a similar theme in many different situations.

RELATIONSHIPS

During the years from nine to twelve, children are very conscious of the importance of belonging and working with a special friend or in small groups. Dance should provide the opportunity for them to continue to enjoy working with each other and guide them toward a greater awareness of the responsibilities and pleasures that can be derived from shared experiences.

Group Relationship to the Teacher

At all ages children enjoy opportunities to respond to the teacher in a movement situation. During these three years the situations should be exciting and challenging. Inherent in the situations provided should be the opportunity for the children to feel themselves identify and move as a group.

Partner and Group Situations

Not all of the following situations can be worked with equal value by both partners and groups. Rising and sinking with a partner can easily become rising and sinking in a group. Making shapes with a partner can be given added challenge and dimension in a group. Mirroring, on the other hand, will be far more effective as partner work. Teachers should consequently examine carefully the presentation of the problem and not simply assume that to do it with a partner, then do it in a group, would provide the desired educational experience.

MEETING AND PARTING   In this situation children simply meet and part using a simple movement problem. *Meet* with suddenness, *part* with sustainment. *Meet* using one action, *part* using another action. These situations particularly help children who are starting dance at a later age. Being with a partner removes much of their anxiety and embarrassment. At the same time the situations can be structured to provide for learning many of the simpler movement concepts.

MEETING AND STAYING   This situation provides an added challenge because when children
TOGETHER   stay together they have to adjust to each other. When they stay together they will develop many of the following situations.

LEADING AND FOLLOWING   These situations frequently use meeting and parting, and meeting and staying together. The emphasis is however changed and one child assumes the responsibilities and qualities of leading, while the other assumes the equal but different responsibilities and qualities of following.

SHADOWING   In shadowing actions, qualities and spatial factors are copied, the
AND MIRRORING   shadow producing identical movements. The teacher may decide to limit the situation, i.e., shadow the time factor. In mirroring, the situation has the limitation of being a face-to-face relationship. In both of the situations the children will be acquiring the ability to *observe* and respond with concentration and sensitivity to another's action and mood.

ACTION AND RESPONSE   Once children can observe each other's actions and have a vocabu-
OR   lary of movement they are in a position to carry out a conversation
CONVERSATION   in movement. This is so similar to verbal conversation that teachers need only to understand this to understand the movement potential. One child states, "I leap towards you and sink down." The other responds, "I sink beside you then roll away."

129

| RELATING TO GROUP SHAPES | Although group shapes can be almost limitless in variety when compounded of many children, there are four fundamental shapes which will clarify the experiences of group shape. |

| AN ARROW OR WEDGE—SHAPED GROUP | The group can be linear or solid but will have the quality of penetrating space or tapering in space. |

| A BLOCK-SHAPED GROUP | This group can be linear or solid and will have the quality of power and strength. |

| A LINEAR-SHAPED GROUP | A line has plasticity and can change its formation from a circle, to a curve, to a snake, to a zig-zag, to a spiral. These can be experienced in sequence or separately. |

| A PLASTIC-SHAPED GROUP | This group is amoeboid, plastic, fluid, ebbing and flowing in its shape. A twisted, tortuous angular shape may give place to a rounded, undulating, globular mass. |

| RELATING TO GROUP ACTION | Children can develop a feeling of belonging to a group by participating in group action, in a jumping group, a spinning group, or shivering group, for example. |

| GROUP EFFORT | Feeling and sensing the mood of a group can be experienced in a sudden group, a lively group, a slow group, a powerful group, a writhing group. |

| GROUP CONTACT | By touching, children can feel physically the sensation of belonging to a group: for example, a rising group using light touch, a sinking group using strong grip. |

130

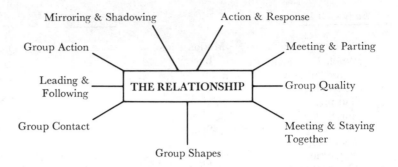

Diagram 5

In all of the above areas of relationship, the children will develop the situation in which they are relating by using material from the area of body, effort, and space. It is essential to give children of this age a functional problem to solve: for example, using a leaping action and a turning action to develop meeting and parting. They cannot simply be told to construct and develop a meeting and parting situation.

During the experience, the teacher will focus upon the learning involved in the relationship area. What does your leap show of your attitude and approach to each other? When you part, is your attention still on your partner or are you leaving and forgetting him? By the correct questioning the teacher can help the children to explore the depths of the relationship.

A Summary of Movement Concepts

Body — What

Activity:
- Whole body actions and stillness
- Travelling
- Turning
- Jumping
- Stopping
- Vibrating
- Percussing
- Contracting
- Expanding
- Sinking
- Rising
- Advancing
- Retreating

Body Parts:
- Used
- Emphasized
- Leading
- Gesturing

Body Shape:
- Wide
- Narrow
- Twisted
- Round
- Symmetrical
- Asymmetrical

Body Zones:
- Upper half
- Lower half
- Right side
- Left side
- Front half
- Back half

Body Base:
- Standing
- Sitting
- Kneeling
- Lying

Body Flow:
- Simultaneous
- Successive

Effort — How

Motion Factor

Energy

Quality
- Strong — firm
- Light — fine touch

Time

- Quick — sudden
- Slow — sustained

Space

- Direct
- Flexible

Flow

- Free
- Bound

Combining Two Motion Factors

Energy & Time

Quality
- Firm and sudden
- Firm and sustained
- Finetouch and sudden
- Finetouch and sustained

Space & Energy

- Direct and firm
- Direct and finetouch
- Flexible and firm
- Flexible and finetouch

Space & Time

- Direct and sudden
- Direct and sustained
- Flexible and sudden
- Flexible and sustained

Combining Three Motion Factors

Energy, Space, Time

Quality
- Firm, direct, sudden
  - *Thrust*
- Finetouch, direct, sudden
  - *Dab*
- Firm, flexible, sudden
  - *Slash*
- Finetouch, flexible, sustained
  - *Float*
- Firm, direct, sustained
  - *Press*
- Finetouch, direct, sustained
  - *Glide*
- Firm, flexible, sustained
  - *Wring*
- Finetouch, flexible, sudden
  - *Flick*

Space — Where	*Relationship — With Whom*
General: Everywhere	**Partner, Trios, Groups** Situations: Leading & following Mirroring Copying Action & response (conversation)
Personal: Located	
Extensions: Large Small	Spatial Relationships: Meeting Parting Splitting Linking Passing Above Below Near Far Beside Around
Levels: High Medium Deep	
Direction: Forwards Backwards Sidewards	
Space Words: Over, under, around Near, far, towards Away from, onto, into Above, below	Spatial Formations: Linear Solid Irregular
Floor Patterns: Straight Angular Closed curve Open curve	Time Relationships: Sudden Sustained Metrical Non-metrical
Air Pattern: Straight Angular Closed curve Open curve	Energy Relationships: Strong, firm Light, finetouch With contact Without contact
Focus: Direction Distance	Mimetic Relationships: Dramatic Relationships:

Table of Suggested Work in Grades 4 to 6

Grade 4	Grade 5	Grade 6
Body		
1. Action words.	1. Master the material for Grade 4.	1. Master the material for Grades 4 and 5.
2. Body parts emphasizing or leading an action	2. Body base: standing / sitting / kneeling / lying	2. Body symmetry and asymmetry
3. Body shape: ball / wall / arrow / twist	3. Body function: bending / stretching / twisting	3. Body zones
	4. Gestures of head and limbs.	
Effort		
1. Distinguish the separate motion factors of time, energy and space.	1. Master the material for Grade 4.	1. Master the material for Grades 4 and 5.
2. Combining two motion factors: a) firm-sudden b) firm-sustained c) flexible-sudden d) flexible-sustained e) direct-sudden f) direct-sustained g) flexible-finetouch h) flexible-firm	2. Combine three motion factors into complete effort actions: a) glide b) float c) flick d) dab e) press f) thrust g) wring h) slash	2. Recognize and work with pairs of opposite effort actions: a) flick — press b) float — thrust c) glide — slash d) dab — wring
		3. Change one motion factor to make a gradual effort transition: a) flick — float = time change b) flick — dab = space change c) flick — slash = energy change

Grade 4	Grade 5	Grade 6
	Space	
Forward	1. Master the material for Grade 4	1. Master the material for Grades 4 and 5
1. Directions: Backward	2. Floor pattern	2. Space words
Sideways	3. Air pattern	3. Advancing and Retreating
High	4. Opening and closing	
2. Levels: Medium		
Deep		
3. Rising and sinking		
	Relationship	

Because relationships can be presented to children simply or completely, according to their stage of readiness, no ordering of the material into specific grades is given.

The foregoing material constitutes much of the discipline of dance which will be acquired during the years from nine to twelve. Naturally the children's background experience and consequent readiness for this material will effect the degree to which it can be studied. These areas will be interwoven one with the other. In this way the children will be acquiring a balance in their movement experiences which will enable them to work in a creative way with many dance ideas. The following table is offered as a guide to the areas which might be covered in each year.

At the outset of the lesson, a unit of work, or a year's program, the teacher must decide very clearly what she hopes will be the outcome of the experience for the children. Naturally she will be looking at this in an educational manner and hoping to affect attitudes, appreciation, social awareness, and the broad goals and values which dance might have. On the other hand, she should be determining quite specific instructional objectives which relate to the content of the material which has to be mastered.

To do this she must determine four things:
1. the desired terminal behaviour which the children should reach,
2. the entering behaviour of the children,
3. the sequence and structuring of the learning experiences,
4. the way in which she can determine whether or not the objectives have been reached.

Using the table the teacher could therefore select the desired area of material to be learned. For example, a Grade 6 class might be asked to master the knowledge of four basic effort actions. During the previous dance lesson the teacher will have assessed their level of readiness for this area of learning. The teacher will then decide how she will sequence and structure the necessary learning experiences. (For ideas on this she can refer to Chapter 2.) At the end of the time unit set aside for this, the teacher must decide whether or not the children have understood, mastered and can create with the four basic effort actions. Upon this knowledge she will determine the next set of instructional objectives.

The successful development of a dance program is dependent upon a clearly structured study of the concepts of movement. The most successful and creative teachers will almost always be found amongst those who have ordered the discipline of dance into a systematic process of learning and teaching.

REFERENCES

Laban, Rudolf. *Mastery of Movement.* London: Macdonald and Evans Ltd., 1960.

6

STIMULI

Many things excite the curiosity, imagination and wonder of children. They will startle you by seeing beauty in something you have long passed by; they will "drop dead" in mortal anguish; or demolish you with their need for scientific detail. In each one there would seem to be an explorer, a scientist and an artist, who can enter into a world and see, smell, touch, hear and feel it with absorption. The growing child is part of the growing world, and his overflow of exuberance and energy makes it possible for him to be constantly enquiring, absorbing, challenging, changing, identifying, demolishing, rebuilding the world both outside of and within himself. His learning grows out of exposure to many things. In dance children can gather and collect rich, exciting and meaningful experiences through the study of varied stimuli.

The term stimuli used in this context relates to verse, story, legend, natural phenomena, topical and historical events, tactile objects, realistic and fantastic ideas, which can be given creative form in dance. The stimulus need not always be serious. It can provide a joke, a laugh and a chuckle, or help the children to feel empathy with the tattered scarecrow and add a further dimension to their understanding of good and evil. Dance in this instance provides the medium for creating, interpreting, imitating and expressing, ideas, feelings, understanding, and knowledge of the everyday world. Using stimuli for dance is different from using pure movements but each have their rightful place in children's dance education.

In presenting stimuli for dance, care should be taken that the material is worthy of having time and attention devoted to it. This means, inevitably, that the teacher is having to make value judgements. This, however, is an essential responsibility of the teacher and there are certain guide lines in dance which can help the teacher in choosing stimuli.

1. Is the stimuli challenging both physically and intellectually?
2. Is the stimuli within the range of the children's ability to comprehend and express the idea, emotion or mood involved?
3. Is the stimuli meaningful for the child in contemporary society?

4. Is the stimuli rich in movement ideas?

The following material offers a few ideas for using and developing stimuli. Behind each idea are countless others which can be discovered by the children and the teacher. Some of the ideas you will like, some you will dislike, but each is presented with the hope that both the teacher and children will become impatient to try their own ideas on dance stimuli.

Finding the Movements in Stimuli

When starting to use stimuli with children, it is very easy to get carried away with excitement over a new idea only to find that in a practical situation it fizzles out. A tree or a flower growing out of the ground often sounds like a good idea to the beginner: The children curl up small, push up through the ground, open their buds or branches to the sun all in the space of a few seconds. The experience can certainly be expanded by exploring which parts of the body lead up from the ground, or sensing the quality of strength of a tree. Even with these additions, the movement experience does not last very long. Little has been done to enrich the children's movement experience, extend their knowledge, evoke their imaginations or excite their interest. The original idea in other words was lacking in sufficient movement potential. Stimuli therefore have to be found which upon critical examination contain:
1. Scope for varied action words and use of body parts,
2. Scope for using changes in time, energy and space,
3. Scope for using different spatial concepts,
4. Scope for individual and group work.
All four of these areas need not be present in equal balance, but the stimuli should allow for development in at least two of the areas. In order to verify the movement potential an outline can be established first, showing the material of the stimuli and the movement content which it contains. From this outline the presentation and guided experiences can be decided upon.

138

NATURAL PHENOMENA

The sea, wind, rocks, clouds, streams, rain, shells, fire, snow can be both a source of wonder and scientific enquiry. Children are often acutely aware of the nature which surrounds them and of which they are a part. Sometimes, they need to be awakened and made receptive to this world. Dance can provide for both of these situations. It can give to children the opportunity to express their oneness with the universe or it can arouse their senses and emotions to the new and unknown in the world of nature. The following material represents one way in which children could be guided in exploring some of the movement potential in natural phenomena.

Spirits of the Earth

In the ballet suite, "The Perfect Fool" by Gustav Holst, one piece of music is aptly named, "Spirits of the Earth". From the stimulus of the name, plus the music, the following group dance evolved with a Grade 6 class. Some parts of the story—the rock, the rain, the stream and the lightning—were also worked out with Grade 4 children. In their interpretation the stream moved very slowly and sluggishly on its stomach towards the rock. The rock, which in some instances was precariously balanced on one leg, was consequently in danger of toppling, touching the lightning and ensuring earthly chaos. Fortunately the stream made it just in time and the spontaneous choreography lasted until the tale was told.

Potential Material	Movement Content
All is dormant but then the spirits of the earth awake.	Whole body actions / rising, leaping, jumping, turning, running. Effort / strong with time changes; sometimes sudden bursts of energy, sometimes sustained rumblings.
The earth lies dormant but stirs slightly when the spirits first try to use their powers upon it.	Shape / individual or group, plastic curled, blocked. Body parts / rising, sinking, opening, closing.
The spirits try again to invoke the earth. This time the earth responds and reacts to the spirits.	Partner or group work / action and response; leading and becoming individuals. following; splitting and
The earth and spirits travel individually but gradually	Whole body actions / turning, travelling, vibrating, leaping.

139

re-form into four types of groups.

These groups depict the rain, the streams, the rocks, the lightning. They group and freeze as stillness settles over the earth.

Group work / Creating group shapes by forming together solid, linear, angular, and plastic formations.

Gradually the earth again starts to move. The rain starts to gently fall and travel over the earth.

Rain / Finetouch, delicate, gentle, with time changes. Travelling hardly touching the ground.

The rain falls into the stream which begins to flow more rapidly. The rain dies away.

Stream / Flexible, increasing in strength. Floor pattern and air pattern are important.

The stream flows, surrounds the rock, causes the rock to move then the stream subsides. The rock moves over the earth, generates the lightning and then is still.

Stream / Continuing of floor and air pattern.
Rock / Strong, percussive, direct group action.
Rock / Direct pathway. Strong, powerful, sudden or sustained actions.

Lightning / Zig-Zag pathways on floor and in air. Sudden and strong actions of body parts.
Lightning, Rain, Rock, Stream / All continue their own characteristic movements. Start slowly and increase in size, strength and time.

The lightning flashes and thunder roars across the sky and its jagged forks again cause the rain, the stream and the rock to start moving. The earth is in tumult.

Gradually the tumult starts to subside, the earth is quieted and the spirits depart.

Body actions / decrease in size and strength of all actions followed by sinking or stillness.

Presentation

When presenting this idea the work may develop over several lessons. During these lessons the children will: i) be given the opportunity to explore all of the parts: earth, spirits, rain, stream, lightning and rock. ii) be given the opportunity to select either the earth or one of the spirits to commence the dance. iii) form a group which represents one of the four phenomena, rain, stream, rock, lightning.

In groups they will have to work out how they will shape their groups and capture the necessary quality of each part of the total action. Several guided experiences will need to be given in each part of the story and some of these are outlined below.

How do the spirits disturb the earth?

1. The children can use any spot on the floor and with leaping, rising, turning actions focus on that spot.
2. Having made contact with the spot through focus and action, they use the whole of their bodies to try to bring that spot to life.

How has the earth settled?

Explore the feeling of being attached to the floor. Parts of the body are anchored. You pull against those anchored parts. They move but then another body part anchors you down.

How do the earth and spirits react to each other?

1. Instead of spots on the floor the spirits now work with a partner. Similarly, the earth now reacts to the spirits.
2. The children can interact with partners or in groups in a spontaneous situation. The spirits try to invoke the earth, it stirs and becomes dormant again.
3. The spirits try again, repeating their leaping, turning, pulling actions and the earth, body parts by body parts, gradually pulls away from the floor.
4. Once the earth has been awoken the spirits and the earth dance in a leading and following situation. This should be a simple sequence worked out between the children and consists of three or four action words. The sequence should portray their idea of how the spirits and the earth would unite in delight at their power and freedom. The sequence might be shiver-whirl-skip-leap.
5. The children leave their partners and continue to travel, using the same sequence of movement.

How do the groups form and establish their characteristics?

The rock	The children join, one by one. They link body parts until they create a solid unmoving rock of any shape.
The stream	The children meet, one by one, and gently link, or touch, body parts to form a linear but curving shape.

| The lightning | The children meet but do not join by touch. Instead they create a zig-zag shape by themselves assuming angular body shape. Each child adds to the length of the zig-zag by his position in the group. |
| The rain | The children meet but again do not join by touch. They select different levels and, with these between them, create a grouping. The essential factor for them is to retain a feeling of lightness and buoyancy as if they have just bounced off the earth. |

How do the groups relate to each other ?

1. By meeting, affecting another group and parting, group relationships are established. The rain, keeping its quality of lightness and by using skipping, bouncing, flicking, dabbing actions, approaches the stream. As it reaches the stream the actions cease and the group returns to stillness.
2. The stream selects a curving pathway which covers a great deal of space. Keeping themselves lightly joined the children swoop, swirl, travel and surround the rock and become still.
3. The rock, using very restricted jumping, hopping, bouncing, stepping action, gradually moves powerfully but with a slow rhythm across the floor to touch the lightning. The rock then freezes to stillness.
4. The lightning, using leaps and slashing movements through the air, travels as a group cutting out zig-zag air and floor patterns. The lightning suddenly splits and the children part from their group. Each one goes to another group and leaping and slashing set them moving.

How does the tumult grow and then cease?

The three remaining groups increase the speed and intensity of their actions until they are forced to split. Each child, as an individual, continues with his actions, gradually decreasing them in size and intensity. A few at a time they sink or assume positions of stillness.

This group dance can be accompanied by the music, "Spirits of the Earth" from the ballet, "The Perfect Fool". The music in this can be used to accompany, not restrict or guide the action. Alternatively, the work can be accompanied by percussion or be danced out in silence.

"Spirits of the Earth" offered the opportunity for work as individuals, in small groups, and for the whole class to join together in a final large group dance. Not all work with natural phenomena needs to be developed in this way. There are many aspects of stimuli which can be worked solely by individuals or in small groups. The following verse by Eleanor Farjeon speaks of natural phenomena which could be very simply developed in this way.

THE TIDE IN THE RIVER

The tide in the river
The tide in the river
The tide in the river runs deep.
I saw a shiver
Pass over the river
As the tide turned in its sleep.

The following prose from *A Sense of Wonder* by Rachael Carson could lead to a whole exploration of things of the sea.

Down on the shore we have savored the smell of low tide—that marvellous evocation combined of many separate odors, of the world of seaweeds and fishes and creatures of bizarre shape and habits, of tides rising and falling on their appointed schedule, of exposed mud flats and salt mire drying on the rocks.

In these years the children will be concerned with the activity, the sense of enquiry, feeling and adventure, associated with natural phenomena. Later they will be able to sense the symbolic which is always present in night and day, and the ebb and flow of nature.

THE PLACE OF VERSE IN CREATIVE DANCE

> It is a fact that, when we are young, poems affect us stir us touch us
> or amuse us or beautifully puzzle us as they never quite do again.[1]

Children can, in movement, become the illustrators of many poems.
This, in essence, is what they become when a poem fires their imagination. They wish to take hold of the poem and make themselves one
with it. They do this by seeping themselves in the poem's story, its
mood, its quality, its life. Then they give it a different life by bring-
ing something of themselves to it as they illustrate it in paint, clay,
drama, words or dance. A whole poem may appeal to the child, or
only one line, or even part of a line. We should give the children
the opportunity to create when they are strongly drawn towards
something.

The following poem was presented to a Grade 4 class of children
with the idea of capturing, with them, the essence and quality of
slowness. Once they had become familiar with this quality, they
became the illustrators of one line which particularly appealed to
them. In order to ensure that the children could understand each
line, the poem was presented both visually and verbally. It is to the
children of Banff Elementary School that I am indebted. Their
interpretation and illustration of each line had the freshness, unique-
ness and total sincerity for which one so often looks and yet seldom
finds.

This poem by James Reeves, can be found in the *Oxford Book of
Poetry for Children*.

SLOWLY

Slowly the tide creeps up the sand,
Slowly the shadows cross the land,
Slowly the cart-horse pulls his mile,
Slowly the old man mounts the stile.

Slowly the hands move round the clock,
Slowly the dew dries on the dock.
Slow is the snail—but slowest of all
The green moss spread on the old brick wall.

[1]Edward Blishen and Brian Wildsmith, *Oxford Book of Poetry for Children*
(London: Oxford University Press, 1963).

Presentation

This poem could be approached in two ways. Each line could be explored by the whole class for its action, it quality and its relationship. In this case all of the children would explore the idea of the tide creeping up the sand, and later of the hands moving round the clock. The alternative is to help all the children explore "slowness" in whole body action, in body parts, in groups, in partners. After they have explored the quality, give them complete freedom in selecting their own line to create an illustration and movements. The latter approach is now considered.

How can we capture the feeling and know about "slowness"?

1. From any position near to the floor, touch the floor very gently with the finger tips. Then equally gently, but very slowly, lift the fingers and touch a different spot on the floor. Repeat this several times feeling the slowness of the action.
2. Try letting the hands meet and part very slowly.
3. On the feet explore stepping very slowly from one place to another.
4. Letting any body part lead the way, explore spreading and narrowing the whole body but retain the slowness of the actions.

After the children have been give time to explore at least some of these activities, read the verse to the children. At the same time, project, or write, the verse so that it is visible. At this point, set the children the following problem:

An artist sometimes illustrates a poem with a sketch or a painting. Today you are going to be the artist but instead of using paper and paints you are going to use movements and paint your illustration in space. Choose the line which you would like to illustrate and then go and find your space in which to paint your illustration.

In most instances all of the children have gone and become quickly absorbed in their own work. A few have needed further help, perhaps a line re-read, some help in selecting. In these instances the teacher has time to work with a few individuals and they too soon become happily absorbed.

THE DANCING RING

Illustrating verse can be one approach to its use in dance. But dance may also complement the verse. Children moving to the sound of the spoken poem, complement and add to its richness. In a similar way, dancer and music often fuse to create a greater richness than either art alone can produce. In the following poems, taken from *A Pepper Pod*, rhythm and words can combine.

BON DANCE

The dancing rings become
Larger and larger to the beat
Of the quickening drum

Or accompanying work with the qualities of firmness and finetouch, this simple verse can be interpreted in dance:

GENTLE WILLOW

Angry, I came home
And found within my garden
A willow-tree

As music, art, sculpture, can blend with, unite, support, stimulate, or accompany dance, so too can verse. The teacher who has a great love of verse and children, is already equipped to explore the medium of creative dance.

CHARACTERIZATION

A child of two busy in the garden helping his father sweep the leaves, or sitting in the driving seat of a sand-made car, is not involved in characterization. He is imitating, identifying, learning about the things his father does. Older children will still imitate, identify, learn from their peers and adults. They are also capable of abstracting the actions, qualities, moods, situations, of groups of people, individuals, animals. Using this knowledge, they can create dance characterizations. With guidance they are able to discover the essential action and quality required for the scarecrow, the puppet, the thief, the genie, the old man, the cat, the deer, the hunter, the witch doctor, and many other characters of both fact and fantasy. They have the knowledge to place these characters in their environment: the hunter in the forest; the genie in the bottle; the puppet in the box. From the knowledge of the character and the situation they can develop the sequence of actions which may occur.

Animals

With characterization, as with all other dance stimuli, the children will need guidance in discovering the movement possibilities. The characterization of the deer could be a dismal failure if the children attempt a literal interpretation, moving on their hands and feet about the room. Instead they can be guided to think about the quality or the effort with which a deer moves. The wonderful bound in the air with the body tense and concentrated. The alert stillness, the startled turn of the head. In capturing these actions and qualities the children will be entering into a deeper understanding and empathy with the deer than could be achieved by superficial mimicry. As Laban so aptly states, "Man's body-mind produces many qualities. He can jump like a deer, and if he wishes, like a cat."[2]

Primitive Gods

Characterizations of the primitive gods of war, harvest, and medicine, would each require a different study and interpretation. The god of war would explore movements which were powerful: strong stepping action; commanding gestures which sweep through the air; leaps and bounds of strength; stillness full of concentration and intensity. The god of medicine would be more devious and subtle in his actions: leaps would have power but the placement of the hands and arms would be suggestive of invoking evil; small

[2]Rudolf Laban, *Mastery of Movement* (London: Macdonald and Evans Ltd., 1960), p. 13.

148

STAMPING, LEAPING, PRIMITIVE GODS

and firm gestures of hands and arms would explore in gripping and releasing actions; facial expressions would be narrowed or widened. The god of harvest would be characterized by the design and repetition of harvesting actions, gathering the corn, gesturing to the sun and the rain with rising, opening, turning actions.

People

The burglar, the clown, the juggler, the acrobat, the sailor, the drunk, the pedlar, the magician, the toy-maker, are all general terms for classes of people. Because of this we can assume they have certain characteristics in common which can be explored in dance. To avoid stereotyping such as, "all sailors walk with a rolling gait", we should encourage the children to look more deeply into the type of character they are portraying. A sailor might be characterized by a sequence of walking actions associated with life on board ship. Certainly the era in which the ship is placed will effect the action. The days of sail provide many different forms of activities from the days of the nuclear submarine. The sailor might be less concerned with action and more with space. Focusing far out to the horizon, above into the skies and below into the sea. Action and space might give way to rhythm, a sailor or a group being characterized by different rhythms which are caused by the effect of the sea upon the ship. Searching into the movement possibilities of the characters will ensure a far richer movement experience for the children than restricting the movement to one stereotyped idea.

Instead of creating dances about a certain type or group of people specific characters can be used as the source of dance stimuli. The character may be fictional or factual but each will have something which makes he or she unique. Florence Nightingale, Long John Silver, St. Joan, Thomas à Becket, The Knights of the Round Table, Lancelot, St. Francis are examples of characters which appeal to the imagination and sense of glory of children. Short but sincere sequences of creative movement or dance which children create from these romantic figures frequently say more than many descriptive verbal passages.

Fables

Jean de la Fontaine in his fables often uses character. The traditional figures of the lion, the fox, the ant, the grasshopper, mountain, sun, and wind are given human characteristics. Several of his fables—"The Stag and the Vine"; "The War of the Rats and the Weasels"; "The Fox who Lost his Tail"—are examples of excellent stimuli for dance. With adaptations being made for the

150

different age groups the following fable can be created with all of the three grades.

The Wager of the Wind and the Sun

The fable tells the story of the wager between the Wind, Boreas; and the Sun, Apollo; to force a traveller to remove his cloak.

> Our voyager passed through the storm serene
> Enveloped in a cloak of sturdy stuff,

The sun and the wind agree:
    To find the one shall make him first undress.
The efforts of the wind were to no avail:

> Our wagering blower
> Gulps in the air, swells like a balloon,
> A raging diabolical typhoon
> Shrieking, roaring, howling; he slates the tower
> And cracks the roof and founders many a ship . . .

The traveller shelters from the wind and so the wind is unsuccessful. The sun then tries his skill:

> Apollo melts the heaven with his fire:
> Warms and revives the traveller with his ray;
> and wins the wager:

> Beneath his cloak he makes the man perspire,
> Compelling him to throw his cloak away.

Potential Material	*Movement Contents*
The wind establishes his character	Body actions / Boisterous leaping actions. Expansive gestures accompanying the leaps. Effort / Strong, lively, with moments of finetouch and suddenness. Space / Uses general space. Filling space with actions and gestures.
The sun establishes his character	Body actions / Rising, opening actions. Turning, revolving, expansive gestures accompanying action. Effort / Strong, direct, interplay between gliding and pressing. Changes with flicking and dabbing. Space / Uses personal space cutting space with actions and gestures.
The traveller establishes his character	Body actions / Turning with gathering and scattering gestures. Walking, turning and pausing.

151

RAGING DIABOLICAL TYPHOON

Space / Focus, looking both near and far. Pathways clear cut but on any chosen design.

The sun and the wind meet and make their wager.	Relationship / Partner work with conversation in movements. Each portraying to the other his powers.
The wind approaches the traveller	Relationship / Partner work with meeting, then action and reactions. The wind takes the lead and the traveller reacts.
The sun approaches the traveller	Relationship / Partner work with meeting, then action and reactions. The sun takes the lead and the traveller reacts.
The traveller discards his cloak and the sun and wind observe the results of their wager.	Relationship / Two and one. Body action / Traveller: turning, scattering gestures, freezes. Sun: Rising, opening gestures, freezes. Wind: Closing, shrinking actions, freezes. Space / Focus for sun and wind on traveller. Traveller focus into distance.

Presentation

The children should be introduced to the story of the fable and given the opportunity for discussing the characteristics of Boreas, Apollo and the traveller.. The unfolding of the events should be established and then movement exploration should begin.

How does the wind establish his character?

1. With eyes closed or open, inhale a large amount of air which makes you feel blown up, then deflate yourself. Repeat this several times.
2. Develop the inhaling into a large action, it might be a leap, a roll, an opening out, a turn, a skip. When you breathe out make this your moment of recovery from the action. For example, leaping and inhaling, landing and exhaling.
3. Reverse the procedure; when you inhale let it be a gathering together of all your forces. Then explode all the air into a run, a whirl, a jump, a slash.
4. Use the idea to create your own "wind sequence" using the

idea of breathing or blowing up as an important part of your character.

5. Keep the words boisterous, blustery, shrieking, roaring, howling in your mind. Try to let your sequence get the feeling of the words. Perhaps a boisterous jump, a shrieking run, or a roaring turn might be what you need.

How does the sun establish his character?

1. Explore a rising spiralling action. Your body is the axis and your arms and hands shape the spiral around you as you rise.
2. Repeat the rising action but make the palms of the hands face outwards and focus into the distance. The action should have the feeling of the sun spreading its warmth outwards.
3. Travel quickly and lightly over the ground with a travelling action. Pause and find an action with the arms which makes them spoke outward from the centre of the body. When they have spoked out bring them back to the centre. Repeat the action several times to produce the effect of rays radiating outward.
4. Create the character of the sun from spiralling, travelling and radiating. Combine the actions in any order.

How does the traveller establish his character?

1. The traveller should establish a travelling pattern which has a repeatable rhythm and floor pattern. For example:

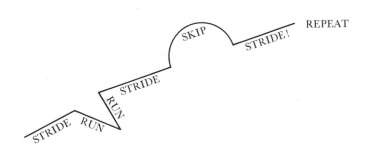

2. Every so often during the travelling pattern, pause and swirl the cloak around yourself, turning as you do this. Make this an important part of the travelling pattern.
3. Give your traveller a mood by having him travel with strength, or lightly and buoyantly. Focusing on the ground beneath or into the distance, looking around or straight ahead.

154

How do the three characters develop the story?

The children, having explored the movement possibilities of all three characters, can now in groups of three select with which one they will work.

In threes they can develop their own interpretation of the sequence of the story. They should be helped by having their attention drawn to the following:

1. The three characters should not be moving all of the time. At times the focus should be on the traveller, at times on the sun and the wind, at others on the wind and the traveller. During these moments the person not in focus should have frozen in an attentive position which relates to the other two.

2. The interplay between the pairs in focus is like a conversation in movement, one speaking and the other replying. These sequences should be short but repeatable.

If this story were being developed with Grade 4 children the teacher might wish to change the presentation to group work. Groups of children taking the parts of the sun, the wind, the traveller. In this way the teacher can guide the story development, so helping the younger ones to achieve a feeling of satisfaction. The Grade 5 and 6 children on the other hand, like the independence of working out their own developments.

MUSIC

Music can accompany dance; the movements and the music growing alongside of each other. This frequently happens when a musician watches how the children are creating their dances and, almost simultaneously, senses their needs and accompanies their work. Music can be found to accompany already created dances or movement sequences, although this is an extremely difficult task. Music can also stimulate an idea for a dance. Music has a universal appeal, but each one of us will be drawn to different music. What will be a source of inspiration for one person may have no effect on another.

Every teacher must select his own library of music. However, the following pieces stimulated certain ideas and are offered as starting points for using music as stimuli for dance.

The Sword: Donaldson

Using both the underlying rhythm and the overlapping melody, the idea developed around the combination of power and gentleness, show that the hands can show both of these qualities. The dance is developed with partners using the palms of the hands to meet, touch and then together create a simple rising and sinking motif. The movements are very clearly developed and the idea is convyed of the ritualism of prayer, worship.

Creatures of the Garden: Donaldson

This piece of music invoked the idea of the spirit who had been buried in the earth for a thousand years. He gradually emerges from his captivity, dances first upon the spot where he was imprisoned, then in delight he dances over all the earth, exploding every so often in the air.

Circus Music: Copland

This piece from the longer work, *Red Pony,* stimulated the idea of a fair ground. Into the story of the fairground was brought the merry-go-rounds, the slides, ball throws, shooting galleries, the room of mirrors, the wrestling ring. The children were all engaged in groups in all of the activities, which developed sequentially, one activity leading into the next.

The Legend of Johnny Pot: Dick Hyman

A scarecrow, torn and tattered, discovers he has life in his hands, then his arms, next his head, legs and whole body. So pleased to find this, he shivers with excitement. He decides to venture step by step into the field and becomes so overjoyed with his legs moving that he starts to dance. Finally, he returns to his responsibility of scaring away the birds and resumes his former shape.

The Workmen's Dance: John Dalby

This piece is Band B of Side 1 of *Music for Dance*. The workmen pick up their shovels, throw them over their shoulder and dance to work. They do this reluctantly, dancing four steps forward to work and immediately four skips backward. After four attempts at this they arrive and start rhythmically shoveling. Again this is somewhat half-hearted. They dig their shovels into the ground and then "flick" the earth over their shoulder, occasionally stopping to wipe their forehead. They exchange this activity for work with the pneumatic drill which makes them vibrate around in a circle. Quickly tiring of this activity they head for home; but instead of going forward and backward they move continually forward but with steps and skips.

The Beauty and the Beast: Ravel

This piece from *The Mother Goose Suite* stimulates a light lilting mood of travelling, skipping, turning, enjoying space which then is changed by sudden thoughts of darkness and evil. An attempt is made not to be drawn towards this darkness. After the conflict of being drawn towards both good and evil the dancer returns permanently to one state or the other.

Alternatively, as the composer intended, the music can accompany the story of the conversation between Beauty and the Beast and the gradual freeing of the Beast from his enchanted spell.

Nights in the Gardens of Spain: De Falla

This is mood creating music stimulated by a simple composition called "Abstract". In groups of three the body is used to create many abstract designs. This abstraction is taken into space and returns again to the group design. Although the complete musical work is not used for this dance, it is possible to fade out the music in such a manner as not to destroy the beauty and meaning of the musical composition.

Below Disco Volante: John Barry

This part of the film score to *Thunderball* suggested and helped to evoke the volcanic disaster. Group work depicted the ever increasing dynamic build up of force within a volcano, the eventual

157

eruptions which took place, the travelling of the lava and ash which submerged a city. The sculptural effects of a new and abstract nature are created from the ruins.

These are but a few of the ideas which may arise from a musical stimulus. It is absolutely essential when working from music, as from any other stimuli, that the teacher apply a rigorous test:

1. Does the music evoke and accompany ideas which have within them the potential for movement?

2. Will the idea allow for active bodily participation; does it have within it material which can be developed in space, in effort and in relationships?

3. Is the music a suitable length, and will it expand and challenge the children's understanding of both movement and music?

4. Are the children into the stage of readiness when they can understand and become involved in the mood, rhythm, idea, emotion, and compositional form which is being studied?

All of these questions must be carefully considered before any selection of music is developed.

TACTILE OBJECTS

Children can touch, stroke, handle, manipulate many types of tactile stimuli. They can feel the smoothness, flexibility and the strength in a piece of sun-baked wood; the suppleness and malleability of a rubber band which can be stretched to a thin vibrating tautness and released to a flexible, writhing, sponge-like mass. They can enjoy the roundness of a plastic hoop and yet make it become a living entity which responds to movements; becoming a bicycle pump, a hole in which to hide, an extension of themselves. Wisely used objects become an extension of the child's moving world, giving him an added medium to explore in dance. The wisdom in using objects has to come from the teacher who must know exactly why certain objects are being explored. To present objects as mere gimmicks or for a change of atmosphere is not justified. Such treatment also does great disservice to a potentially educative medium. For objects to have any real value in the child's dance education they should be presented for one of the following reasons:

1. They spark off a greater use of movement imagination than could be achieved solely through a movement approach. The rubber band, which is actually seen, handled, explored for its own movement possibilities, can help the child explore tension and shape. In this instance, the object, itself, can be made to move in many ways.

2. They spark off a greater understanding of quality which can be translated into a deeper movement experience. For example, the razor-like edges of an oyster shell help to produce an understanding of how to bring about angularity and razor-like surfaces in the quality of an action.

3. They heighten the use of imagination in exploring a completely new movement idea or situation. A newspaper becomes something to read, to hide behind, to skate upon, to roll into a sword, to wear as a hat, to come out of the printing press.

Such a careful examination of the movement possibilities of the objects should be made prior to their presentation to the children. Children may wish to bring objects of their own to work with in class. Again they must be helped to find the real movement experience provided by the object.

> Hard but pliable, slender but strong, linear but form producing, wire is another image that children easily comprehend and with which they readily identify. Wire, unlike clay, has not plasticity. Although it can assume an endless number of shapes, its dominant feature is hardness, and each shape is related to, yet always distinct from the next.[3]

---

[3] Jack Wiener and John Lidstone, *Creative Movement for Children* (New York: Van Nostrand Reinhold Company, Inc., 1969).

RELATED YET DISTINCT

Here the image of wire can readily be changed for the reality. The reality, on the other hand, might restrict rather than enrich the children's movement exploration. If objects are seen to be restricting and hampering the children, then they should be discarded. On the other hand, "restricting" must be distinguished from "disciplining." If the objects are enhancing the discipline of the movement as well as extending the range of the movement then they should be used.

Different forms of stimuli have been discussed and each will have a different appeal for children and teachers. Familiarity with a stimulus will help the teacher to feel more secure in the presentation. Unknown aspects should also be considered for they may prove to be a tremendous source of enjoyment for both the teacher and the children.

Dance should not close children in but lead them out in many different directions; some of these directions will be found in together exploring stimuli.

REFERENCES

Bruce, Vi. *Dance and Dance Drama in Education.* New York; Pergamon Press Ltd., 1965.

Laban, Rudolf. *Mastery of Movement.* London: Macdonald and Evans Ltd., 1960.

Murray, Ruth and Lovell. *Dance in Elementary Education.* New York: Harper and Row, Inc., 1963.

SOURCES OF STIMULI

Blishen, Edward, and Brian Wildsmith. *Oxford Book of Poetry for Children.* London: Oxford University Press, 1963.

Carson, Rachael. *The Sense of Wonder.* New York: Harper and Row, Inc., 1956.

La Fontaine, Jean. *The Complete Fables of La Fontaine.* London: New English Library Ltd., 1962.

Wiener, Jack, and John Lidstone. *Creative Movement for Children.* New York: Van Nostrand Reinhold, Company Inc., 1969.

Yasuda, Kenneth. *A Pepper Pod: Classic Japanese Poems Together with Original Haiku by Shoson* (Kenneth Yasuda). New York: Alfred A. Knopf, 1947.

MUSIC REFERENCES

1. "Spirits of Earth" from the ballet *The Perfect Fool* by Gustav Holst, found on the *Adventures in Music Series.*
2. "The Sword" by Donaldson, from the *Children's Rhythms in Symphony.*
3. "Creatures of the Garden" by Donaldson, from the *Children's Rhythms in Symphony.*
4. "The Legend of Johnny Pot" by Dick Hyman, from *Moog, The Electric Electics of Dick Hyman.*
5. "Circus Music", from the *Red Pony* by Copland, found on the *Adventures in Music Series.*
6. "Below Disco Volante", from *Thunderball.* John Barry United Artists 4132.
7. "Beauty and the Beast", from the *Mother Goose Suite* by Ravel.
8. "Nights in the Gardens of Spain" by De Falla.
9. "Music for Dance B1", composed by John Dalby, directed by Valerie Preston-Dunlop. Selection used: "Moving on".

FURTHER MUSIC REFERENCES

1. *Kaleidoscopic Vibrations.* Perrey and Kingsley. Vanguard VSD 79264.
2. *Pure Electronic.* John Gage, Luciana Berio Mimaroglue. Turnabout TU 40461, TV 340465.
3. *In Sound from Way Out.* Perrey and Kingsley. Vanguard VSD 79222.
4. *The Good the Bad and the Ugly.* Sound Track. Hugo Montenegro. Ennio Morricone, composer. U.A. 5172.
5. *A Fistful of Dollars.* Sound Track. Ennio Morricone. LSO 1135, United Artists.

7

TEACHING TECHNIQUES

There are certain fundamental factors which help determine a dance lesson as a satisfying and meaningful experience for children and teacher. The relationship between the children and the teacher must be a satisfactory one for all concerned. This is something which each teacher must resolve in his own way.

From this foundation should be built an enjoyment for the subject of creative dance. However, this can only be acquired by a willingness on the part of the teacher to become interested in the subject, knowledgeable about the content of discipline, and a skilled teacher of movement.

Certain skills or techniques of teaching dance are acquired through practice. Each individual will use a variety of similar techniques or use one which he alone finds successful. Despite the variations which will occur because of different teaching styles, there are points of teaching which can aid the teacher who is starting to teach dance. These will be dealt with in the following order:
1. Teaching Objectives and Observation.
2. The Teacher's Movement.
3. Using Teaching Space.
4. Accompanying Dance.
5. Using Transparencies and Colour Charts.

Objectives and Observation

In order to teach a discipline of dance it is essential to acknowledge that there is a body of knowledge relating to this discipline, which must be grasped. This body of knowledge will provide the instructional objectives for a lesson, a series of lessons, a program for one year and for several years. A lesson designed to help the children acquire the ability to distinguish and use floor patterns and air patterns states an *instructional objective*.

In achieving the instructional objective certain procedures will be used. These methods will be chosen for their educational value in a specific situation. The method produces certain responses be-

163

tween the children and teacher which create an educational situation. At the moment in which the children respond to the teacher in the close-contact situation (in the give and take of a movement or verbal situation), and learning is taking place, then an *educational objective* is being achieved. The teacher will have selected the close-contact grouping because at that time she may wish to strengthen the teacher-children contact and reinforce the learning situation. She is headed towards her objective, has selected a method, and is involved in an educational objective. Furthermore, to ensure that this has been achieved, the teacher must be able to test her method through discussion or observation. "Learning has been defined as a relatively permanent change in a behavioral tendency, the result of reinforced practice."[1]

At the outset of a lesson a teacher should have a very clear idea or plan of the *instructional objectives* of the lesson. Too frequently dance teaching is left to the hope that a vaguely defined educational happening will occur during a lesson. This is understandable because it is extremely difficult to measure dance achievement. One slips into the trap of being vague about what one hopes to achieve, knowing that measurement is virtually impossible. For example, if in putting together a sentence of actions the teacher *observes* that the children are pausing between each word, rather than moving smoothly from one action to the next, then she will concentrate upon this part. She has used observation to make a measurement of performance and has proceeded from her observations.

The skill of observation is not simply one of seeing. It is also one of feeling, knowing, and analysing. Seeing a rising action is not too difficult. Feeling the rising action demands participation and empathy; knowing the rising action means knowing how it is being executed; and, analysing the action means being able to look at its separate parts. The teacher has to develop each one of these skills of observation and use each one at a different time for a different purpose.

Observing by seeing

Seeing is more than looking. Seeing requires attention and concentration. When we begin teaching, we only see a very small part of the children's movements. As we use and develop the skill we see more and for longer periods of time. To develop the skill some decisions have to be made about delineating the viewing areas. A

[1]John P. DeCecco, *The Psychology of Learning and Instruction* (New Jersey: Prentice-Hall, Inc., 1968), p. 248.

teacher may decide to observe, generally, the whole class, or concentrate for a few seconds on one child. She may decide to concentrate on seeing how the children use space, or whether they have really understood meeting. She may decide to observe a sentence of action. (But to observe and retain a long sentence of movement is as difficult as hearing and retaining a long verbal sentence.) The teacher could concentrate upon seeing parts of the sentence, always remembering to look at the beginning, the middle and the end; not always and only the beginning. This requires awareness. Sometimes there may be a need to observe with minute accuracy. This is observing through analysing.

Observing by analysing

This is a development of observing by seeing. In this instance, the movement is broken down into its smallest parts and analysed in terms of the action, the space, the dynamics, and the relationship. A gesture of the arm would include an analysis of all the *parts* of the arm including the hand, as well as the *whole* arm and hand. Questions the teacher should ask:
1. "Did the arm show a gathering (inward) or scattering (outward) action?"
2. "Was the action performed simultaneously by all parts of the arm or did one part lead?"
3. "What pathway did the arm follow?" Such observation will give an exact analysis of what happened when the arm was moved. It brings the teacher and the children's attention to detail.

From the analysis of the movement content in Chapter 5 the teacher can construct questions which relate to observing through seeing and analysis. The questions should ask:
1. What is the body doing?
2. What time and energy and space factors are being used?
3. Where is the action going in space?
4. What relationships are occurring?
The questions apply to the four major areas of movement analysis: the body, the effort, the space, and the relationships.

It is from these four facets of observation that the teacher will construct his instructional and educational objectives. Observation of the children's total performance is the only guide he has as to their readiness to proceed to the next stage of the lesson or program.

Observing by feeling

Observing by feeling does not negate the fact that first you must look. Instead of looking and emphasizing the seeing, this form of observation emphasizes the feeling. You can watch a child performing, or a group performing, a simple rising action. You are aware not so much of the actual physical activity of seeing, but of all your senses being heightened and you are feeling the rising. This form of observation might be termed empathetic observation. At the end of the action or sequence of actions you can recall bodily what has occurred, although visually you cannot recall it in detail. Teachers may frequently get caught up in this type of observation, particularly when the whole class is involved in unison activity. Some teachers will in fact have a stronger tendency towards this form of observation. When observing in this manner, the questions you ask will be orientated towards: "What was the sensation of the action?" "What was the mood or spirit of the dance?" "What was the rhythm and tempo of the movement?" Here in particular you may "feel yourself understand" what the children are saying in movement.

Observing by knowing

Knowing what had to occur can often fill in observation gaps. For example, knowing that a skip is a combination of a hop and step, the teacher can observe and see if this is actually happening. Knowing that when starting partner work, children will usually dance very close together, makes observation of this fact both simple and confirmatory. Knowing can therefore precede observation and make observation that much easier.

Knowing includes within it previous learning, and observing by knowing makes one anticipate what will occur. This is a daily event in the dance lesson. Observing children running and always selecting a forward clockwise direction should forewarn teachers that if they set a running activity this will occur. A suggestion to change direction usually results in children running around in an anti-clockwise direction. This can be observed time and time again. Yet, *knowing* this does not prevent the teacher from setting the situations which create it. In these situations, knowing and observing are being used negatively; no learning is taking place. All observation should be used as a positive teaching and learning situation. Knowing what will be observed should help the teacher construct the positive, not the negative, learning situation. The questions should be: "What has my observation taught me?" "What do I know from previous observation?"

The Teacher's Movement

Studying the movement content of dance can give teachers an insight into their own movement preferences, habits, selections and how these effect other people, and, in particular, children. Once you know how you move you are in a better position to use movement as a positive teaching aid. This is particularly true in creative dance where children very quickly start to absorb the actions and qualities, and spatial preferences of a teacher. If the children are not to have the stamp of the teacher placed upon them, the teacher must consciously strive to balance her own movement patterns, at the same time not losing her own individuality or movement style. Some questions which you can ask yourself, or ask another teacher to observe and answer for you, will help you to detect your movement preferences:

Time / How do I use time? Am I consistently sudden, slow, in-between? Do I vary my use of time?

Energy / How do I use force? Are all my actions strong, powerful, forceful? Are they all light, delicate? Do I have any attitude towards energy or are my actions weak? Do I vary the use of my energy?

Space / How do I use space? Are my actions flexible, meandering in space? Are my actions direct, linear in space? Do I vary the use of space?

Flow / How do I use the flow of movement? Are my actions continuous? Do they stop and start giving an interrupted appearance?

167

Do I vary the flow of my actions?

These questions, which all belong to the area of effort, show the bias in your own attitude towards movement. If you yourself are consistently and persistently quick, flexible, interrupted, and you wish the children to explore the feeling and sensation of sustainment, directness and continuous flow, then you will need to discipline yourself to produce these actions, be it in the voice or the body. Changing the factors of time and energy will change the tempo and mood; changing the space will change the concentration and attention; changing the flow will change the communication. A skilful and effective teacher may move little and consequently her own movement will have little effect on the children. But her voice and her attitude may be full of movement. A teacher may have an inner feeling for movement, which although not given form in her own movement, comes into the movement of the children she teaches. It is not a question of "physician heal thyself", but of "teacher know thyself".

Using Teaching Space

Directing the Flow of Movement

An awareness of how to use space when teaching creative dance can help in directing the flow of movement and is useful in simple class management.

a) *From the centre of the room.* When the teacher is guiding any *travelling class activity* with the voice or with percussion a central position will create a "whirlpool" of movement. The teacher's space becomes her territory and the children move around the outside usually in a circular pattern.

This may be desired by the teacher, but if not, she should be aware that it is her position which is creating that particular flow of movement.

When the teacher is guiding any activity which *radiates in and out* in a spoke-like formation, the central position helps the flow of movement.

When the teacher is guiding any activity which does not travel, the central position focuses the children's attention to the centre.

The central position then is a very dominant one and should be used as a teaching tool. The teacher should know precisely what will be the effect of that position and why she is using it.

b) *From the sides and corners.* These positions allow the floor space to be completely free. Such a position will help in *travelling activities.* The children then feel free to use all of the space and to create different patterns on the floor.

In non-travelling activities these positions bring some children very close to the teacher and leave some far away. Distance can often be equated with contact and interest in the children. If the children are working with an action in which the teacher desires some form of copying and accuracy then these positions help. All of the children are seeing the action from a similar viewpoint and their attention is focused on the teacher and not on each other.

Using all of the space

At times a teacher will speak, use percussion, or move, teach, from a certain position. She should consequently be aware of from where she is working and its effect. The majority of the time the teacher should be observing and moving into different places as the need arises. Her moving patterns can cut the space, surround the space, take her near to or far from the children. She can work at their spatial level, be above or below them. Although these things will happen spontaneously they should not be random. Approaching a child can give him security, steady him, interest him. Leaving a child can give him time to work on his own ideas, free him from embarrassment, incite him to mischief.

An aware and knowledgeable teacher will use space not as a vacuum but as a positive teaching environment.

Accompanying Dance

For children participating in dance, the sound which they hear accompanying their movements will have a profound effect.

The first and most important accompaniment for dance is the teacher's voice. This must be used to advantage: Not only should the speaking of words suggest and evoke quality, mood, action; but all the various clicking, rounded, percussive, whispering sounds of which the voice is capable, should be fully explored.

Following upon the voice are the sounds which are produced by percussion: These sounds may suggest, command, dictate, bore, excite, control, free, irritate, soothe, be well-timed or ill-timed. Acquiring sensitivity and skill in accompanying movement is essential. This can be achieved by not restricting one's use of the tambour or percussion instrument to only the dance lesson, but by frequently using a drum and spending a few moments practising. In practising the following knowledge about the tambour will help.

169

The tambour

1. Ensure that the skin has been tightened to give a good resonant sound.

2. Use a sheepskin beater which in its softness and resilience produces a more sensitive sound.

3. Carry both the drum and the beater with a light grip in a relaxed position so making it a part of yourself.

4. *Practice drills:*

a) Continuous beats of varying strengths which can accompany running, rising, sinking, opening, closing actions;

b) a short light quick beat followed immediately by a stronger one which can accompany skipping, jumping, freezing, hopping, galloping actions;

c) combinations of beats and strengths, e.g., a continuous succession of beats increasing and decreasing in volume followed by two loud interspersed beats. This could accompany turning with opening and closing followed by two strong sinking actions.

d) use both ends of the beater, the soft end on the skin of the tambour the handle on the sides. (This will give variety in rhythms and quality of sound. Do not use the stick on the skin of the drum as this will produce wear and break the skin);

e) rubbing the hand, knuckles, fingers on the drum to make a soft swishing sound to accompany whirling, turning, creeping, rolling actions;

f) rapidly and lightly using the finger nails on the skin to produce shivering, shaking, vibratory actions;

g) accompany various sentences of different actions before working with the children; e.g., rising, freezing, running, exploding.

Although the tambour is a most versatile and useful instrument for accompanying dance, other percussion should be used. A knowledge of the types of sounds produced by the percussion will avoid such errors as hitting the cymbal loudly and discordantly to produce freezing. Such mistakes can destroy the quality of the lesson and with foresight can be avoided.

Percussion Instruments and Sounds

Cymbals, finger cymbals, triangles, chime bars all produce a ringing sound. Once struck, the sound from these instruments continues to be heard and a *succession of beats* can accompany rising, sinking, opening, closing, turning actions. *A single beat* will produce a sound which starting with volume gradually decreases until it falls again into silence. The lingering quality of these sounds accompanies many impulsive yet delicate actions; a gesture of the arm which lifts, cuts through space, pauses, and lifts again on a fresh sound.

It is this wave of sound (plus the quality of sound) which is so important in the using of ringing instruments.

Claves and rhythm sticks produce percussive sounds in a similar manner to the tambour. However these sounds, because they are produced by wood upon wood, have a lighter, gayer mood. Although they can accompany many of the same actions as the tambour they produce an angularity and sparkle to the actions. For children they also have the advantage of being very easy to handle, becoming a very short extension of the hands.

Marracas, jingle sticks and bells produce the shivering, vibratory sounds of percussion and accompany the very light repetitive actions of shivering, shaking, quivering. The major disadvantage of these instruments being that it is almost impossible to keep them quiet when sound is not required.

The tambourine combines the percussive sounds of the tambour and the shivering sounds of the jingle sticks. It can be an exciting instrument to use but can have serious disadvantages as a teaching instrument. When beaten the vibratory sounds are always heard. This not only makes for a "noisy" atmosphere but blurs the clarity of the percussive sound.

Children enjoy percussion but they should be helped to use it to enhance, not detract, from their movements. The actions and the sound belong together although they may not occur simultaneously. It is the quality of the sound that the children will be hearing, and it is the ability to select the action and quality appropriate for the sound that they must first develop.

Transparencies and Colour Charts

One of the major problems in dance teaching is how to establish an environment which has both structure and freedom. A teacher can establish the structure of a sentence of action words, toss—perch —twirl, and then allow the children to explore their own variations, (See Chapter I). In this situation he has structured the three words and the freedom is in the treatment they are given. But to give greater freedom in the original structure is more difficult if only the spoken word is used. The present the children with a string of words and expect them to remember them long enough to select a sentence is extremely difficult. At this stage they need visual help. Transparencies or colour charts are the most effective because once made they are always available. Colour can, for example, be super-imposed on the transparency, which provides an instant visual classification for the children, and at the same time gives the teacher an opportunity to structure a richer experience.

171

Chart 1

Chart No. 1 uses action words. Many can be made with different numbers of words upon them.

TRAVELING Actions

Run .... Slither

Skip .... Hop

Creep .... Gallop

Pounce .... Dart

RED

STOPPING Actions

Freeze

Perch

Anchor

Grip

BLUE

SINKING Actions

Collapse

Lower

Sink

Fall

YELLOW

TURNING Actions

Spin

Whirl

Swivel

Whip

GREEN

PERCUSSIVE Actions

Stamp

Explode

Punch

Pound

ORANGE

Movement problems relating to the transparency can be:
a) Make a sentence from one red, one blue, and one green action.
b) Make a sentence using all five colors.
c) Explore three "orange" words.
The teacher is still presenting an environment and a structure but the choice has been considerably widened.

Chart 2

Chart No. 2 has within it a greater degree of structure than Chart No. 1.

```
FALL ................. ROLL ................. RISE ................. SHIVER
                                                            BLUE
TREMBLE ......... FREEZE ........... DART ............... EXPLODE
                                                            GREEN
ANCHOR .......... RELEASE ......... RUSH .............. LEAP
                                                            RED
```

Movement problems relating to this transparency:
a) Select a sentence to develop into a short dance sequence.
b) Rearrange one of these sentences into three different sequences.

Chart 3

With transparencies and charts, as with everything else, the teacher must decide what it is that is desired. An exposure to many things, or an exposure to few things.

The following are designed to be used by the teacher to meet objectives relating to space and group work.

BLUE	YELLOW
GREEN	RED
ORANGE	PURPLE

Movement problems relating to Chart No. 3:

a) In a group of five select one pattern and find several ways of creating the feeling and shape of that pattern.

b) Work at the orange and red designs in groups. Find words to describe the sensation of each design.

Effort Actions

Charts 4 and 5

These are designed to help the children to use the eight basic effort actions. The firm actions are placed below the finetouch actions in order to help the children perform these actions in their associated space, high or deep. Each transparency or chart is read from left to right. Read "A" as one complete sentence of effort actions and "B" as another.

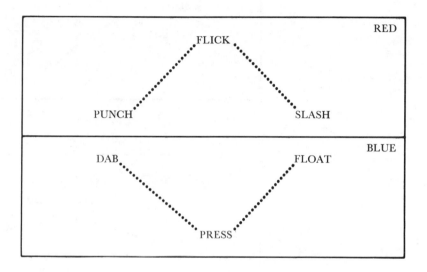

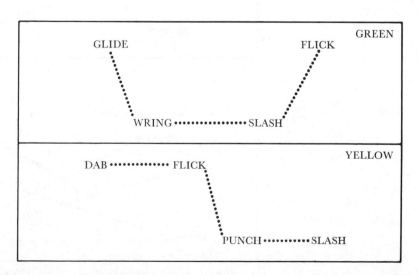

These are designed to show pairs of opposite effort actions. Four effort actions combine to make two pairs. Eight effort actions combine to make four pairs.

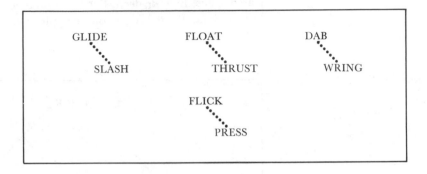

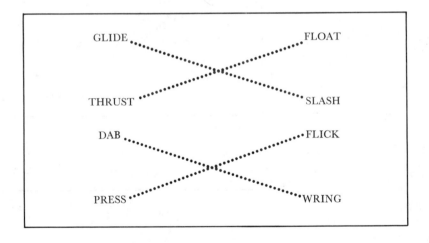

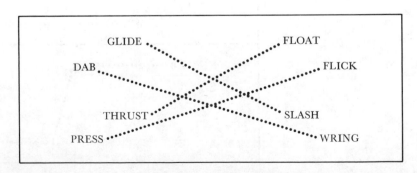

Chart 9

This is designed to give children a visual picture of effort transitions.

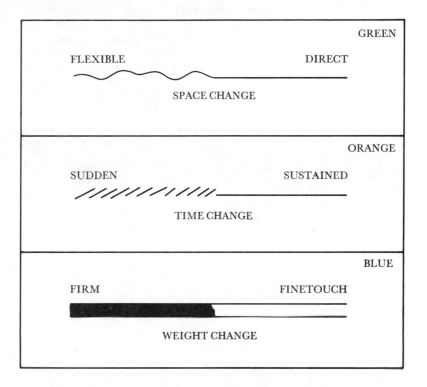

Movement Problems relating to Chart 9.

a) Select the green, orange or blue chart and create a sentence of action.

b) Create a rhythmical sentence of action by repeating three times the orange chart.

c) Create a sentence of action and then record it. e.g.

NOTE

The use of these colour charts or transparencies always presupposes some work with the teacher; e.g., exploring action words, designs, sentences, prior to their presentation.

Several forms of charts can be used and those given previously are examples of how some might be designed. They are but a few of the ideas which can be developed for transparencies and charts. The use of these can give a much greater freedom to the structure of the lesson by allowing children to work at different problems relating to the charts. This form of visual media can help to relate creative dance to the rest of the school curriculum.

These then are some of the practicalities of dance teaching. There are many others. As teachers, we may at times lose sight of such pragmatic factors. But it would seem that the true teacher for generations has not lost sight of the children as he has endeavored to:

> Let each become all that
> He was created able of being.
> Expand, if possible, to his full growth,
> And show himself at length
> In his own shape and stature,
> Be these what they may.

Thomas Carlyle

APPENDIX A

POETRY REFERENCES

BLISHEN, Edward and Brian Wildsmith, *Oxford Book of Poetry for Children,* Oxford University Press, 1963.
"The Tide in The River" — Eleanor Farjeon
"The Eagle" — Alfred, Lord Tennyson
"Slowly" — James Reeves
"I Saw a Peacock with a Fiery Tale" — Anon.
"Winter, The Huntsman" — Osbert Sitwell
"Cat" — Eleanor Farjeon
"The Hag" — Robert Herrick

SANDBURGH, Carl, *Harvest Poems: 1910-1960,* New York: Harcourt, Brace and World, Inc., 1960.
"Sunsets" — Carl Sandburg
"Fog" — Carl Sandburg

ELIOT, T. S., *Old Possum's Book of Practical Cats,* London: Faber and Faber, 1969.
"Macavity: the Mystery Cat"
"Of the Awfull Battle of the Pekes and the Pollicles"

The Penguin Book of Religious Verse, London: Penguin Books Ltd., 1963.
"Prospice" — Robert Browning
"The World" — Kathleen Raine

Japanese Haiku Series, New York: Peter Pauper Press.
There are many selections of Haiku poetry that make excellent starting points for dance, here are mentioned but a few. They are noted by the first line of each poem.
"Ah roadside scarecrow"
"Yellow butterfly"
"Bitter broken reeds"
"Feeble feeble sun"
"As lightning flashes"
"As I light the lamp"
"With the moon-rising"
"Every single star"
"Bitter winter wind"
"In icy moonlight"
"Silly hailstones"
"Ah the falling snow"
"With a whispering hiss"
"A leaf is falling"
"Hop out of my way"
"Scarecrows are the first"

179

"When the tight string"
"Leaf falling on leaf"

O'DWYER, A. AND WHITNEY, G. (Editors) *Fluid Filosofies of Future Fools,* Edmonton: Professional Printing Ltd., 1969.
"War" — Margaret Ohots (Grade 7)
"Disaster" — Linda Blanchet (Grade 9)
"Death" — Shawny Matwichuk (Grade 8)
"The Eagle" — Catherine Brooks (Grade 8)
"The Wind" — Gary Corrigal (Grade 8)
"Snow" — David Parker (Grade 9)

STOKES, Edith M., *World Pictures as a Stimulus for Creative Dance,* London: Macdonald and Evans Ltd., 1970.
"The Fire"
"The Stream"
"The Volcano"
"The Prisoner"

WHITE, Tessa, *Visual Poetry for Creative Interpretation,* London: Macdonald and Evans Ltd., 1969.
"Mirrored"
"Age"
"Autumn Leaves"
"The Blob"
"Conversation"

Miscellaneous selections of poems.
"Drinking Fountain" — Ethel Jacobson
"November Night" — Adelaide Crappey
"Storm" — R. Sue Criss
"April Shower" — Emily H. Watson
"Flicks and Flashes" — Clarence Allen

Poetry provides us with a ready source of stimuli for dance. The foregoing collection of poems presents only a small gleaning from the storehouse of poems available to us. Children should also be encouraged to compose their own poems. These might arise from their own personal experience and involvement in dance, or, having been written as an outgrowth of a different experience, be translated into dance. For further ideas relating to the ways of using words as a stimulus for dance, teachers are referred to:

STOKES, Edith M., *World Pictures as a Stimulus for Creative Dance,* London: Macdonald and Evans, 1970.

APPENDIX B

BOOK REFERENCES

Boorman, Joyce, *Creative Dance in the First Three Grades,* Don Mills: Longmans Canada, 1969.

Bruce, Vi, *Dance and Dance Drama in Education,* New York: Pergamon Press Ltd., 1965.

Carroll, Jean and Peter Lofthouse, *Creative Dance for Boys,* London: Macdonald and Evans Ltd., 1969.

Laban, Rudolf, *Modern Educational Dance,* Second Edition, London: Macdonald and Evans Ltd., 1963.

———, *Mastery of Movement,* London: Macdonald and Evans Ltd., 1960.

Lofthouse, Peter, *Dance,* London: Heinemann Educational Books Ltd., 1970.

Preston, Valerie Dunlop, *A Handbook for Modern Educational Dance,* London. Macdonald and Evans Ltd., 1963.

———, *Practical Kinetography Laban,* London: Macdonald and Evans Ltd., 1969.

Russel, Joan, *Modern Dance in Education,* London: Macdonald and Evans Ltd., 1958.

———, *Creative Dance in the Primary School,* London: Macdonald and Evans Ltd., 1964.

———, *Creative Dance in the Secondary School,* London: Macdonald and Evans Ltd., 1969.

Stokes, Edith M., *Word Pictures as a Stimulus for Creative Dance,* London: Macdonald and Evans Ltd., 1970.

White, Tessa, *Visual Poetry for Creative Interpretation,* London: Macdonald and Evans Ltd., 1969.

All of the above texts are available from:
Canadian F.D.S. Audio Visual,
185 Spadina Avenue,
Toronto 2B, Ontario.

Andrews, Gladys, *Creative Rhythmic Movement for Children,* New York: Prentice Hall, Inc., 1954.

Hawkins, Alma, *Creating Through Dance,* New Jersey: Prentice Hall, Inc., 1964.

Murray, Ruth Lovell, *Dance in Elementary Education,* New York: Harper and Row Inc., 1963.

Wiener, Jack and John Lidstone, *Creative Movement for Children,* New York: Van Nostrand Reinhold Company, Inc., 1969.

APPENDIX C

MUSIC REFERENCES

Although selecting music for creative dance is a very personal operation, most teachers and schools are anxious to start building their own library of records for creative dance. Many of the following records have already been referred to in the chapters of this book; these and others, which have been found to be of tremendous value, are indexed here for ease of reference. All of these records can be purchased from Canadian F.D.S. Audio Visual. Many short selections of music are contained on each record.

Children's Rhythms in Symphony .... L.P.

La Nursery .... E.P.

Electric Sound Patterns . . . by Daphne Oram .... E.P.

Listen, Move and Dance, No's. 1 and 2 .... E.P.'s

The Rhythm Program, Volumes I, II and III .... E.P.'s
    Sets of four records available in sets or separately

The Listening Programs, Volumes I to VI .... E.P.'s
    Sets of four records available in sets or separately

The Listen and Move Series (Green Label)
    A series of eight records available in sets or separately

The Modern Dance Series (Red Label)
    A series of four records available in sets or separately

A Pageant of Dances (Blue Label)
    A series of two records, also available separately